*Discourses delivered to Swamis and Ananda Samajis of the
Nithyananda Order all over the world*

The meditation techniques included in this book are to be practiced only under the direct supervision of an ordained teacher of Nithyananda Dhyanapeetam and in consultation with your personal physician to determine your fitness and ability to do the techniques. They are not intended to be a substitute for medical attention, examination, diagnosis or treatment. If someone tries these techniques without prior participation in the meditation programs of Nithyananda Dhyanapeetam and without the direct supervision of an ordained teacher of Nithyananda Dhyanapeetam, they shall be doing so entirely at their own risk; neither the author nor Nithyananda Dhyanapeetam nor Nithyananda Publishers shall be responsible for the consequences of their actions.

Published by:
Nithyananda Publishers
Nithyanandapuri, Off Mysore road
Bidadi – 562 109, Bengaluru
Karnataka state, India

Copyright ©2009 – 'Living Enlightenment' year

First Edition: May 2008, 1000 copies
Second Edition : October 2008, 2000 copies
Third Edition: June 2009, 1000 copies
Fourth Edition: November 2009, 1000 copies

ISBN 13: 978-1-60607-006-2   ISBN 10: 1-60607-006-1

ll rights reserved. No part of this publication may be reproduced, or stored in a retrieval system, or transmitted by any form or by any means, electronic, mechanical, photocopying, recording or otherwise, without written permission of the publisher. In the event that you use any of the information in this book for yourself, the author and the publisher assume no responsibility for your actions.

All proceeds from the sale of this book go towards supporting charitable activities.

Printed in India by

Judge Press
97, Residency Road, Bangalore - 560 025, Karnataka state
Ph: +91 80 2221 1168   Email: judgepress@gmail.com

You Can Heal
Nithya Spiritual Healing

Nithyananda

Published by **Nithyananda Publishers**

Contents

Heal The Universe 15

Introduction to Healing 28
    What is Healing? 28
    Arogya or Good Health 29
    Healing at the Physical, Mental and
    Emotional Levels 29
        Emotional Healing 30
    History of Healing 30
    Patanjali's System of Healing 32
    Chakras - Subtle, Powerful Energy Centers 33
    Proof of Chakras through Kirlian
    Photography 33
    Chakras and Emotions 35
    Man by Nature is Bliss 36
    The Power of Thought 37
    Body Intelligence 38
        Control of the Senses is Not Needed 38
        Intelligence Down to the Cellular Level 41
        The Power of Self-contradiction 42
    Matter-Energy Equivalence - The Basis of
    Energy Healing 43
    Who Can Give Energy? One Who Has
    Realized He Is Energy 45
    Who Can Receive Energy? 46
    The Person with an Open Heart and Mind 46
    Intellectual Growth Coupled with
    Emotional Growth 48
    The Placebo Effect 51

Placebo effect 51
Nocebo Effect 53
Why Does The Placebo Effect Work? 53
Shraddha 54

Introduction to Nithya Spiritual Healing Initiation 56

Real Courage is the Courage to Face Oneself 57
Dakshinamurthy Swamigal 57
Healers' Initiation - A Marriage between
You and the Divine 59
Healing - A Means to Go Beyond Your Ego 60
    Handling Name and Fame 61

Responsibility – The Way To Expand! 64

State, Not Status 66
Compassion Expresses as Responsibility and Hence
Energy 66
A Cognitive Shift 68
A Commitment to Serve People 70
Ego versus Responsibility 72
Healers are My Hands 73
Responsibility is Not Seriousness - The World is
But a Dream 73

What is Nithya Spiritual Healing Initiation? 76

What is Nithya Spiritual Healing Initiation? 76
Genesis of Nithya Spiritual Healing 76
First Healing Experience 76
The Divine Revelation of the Nithya Spiritual
Healing Formula 77

    Ananda Gandha Chakra 78
    Enter the Space Within 79
    Ananda Gandha in the Context of the
    Chakra System 79
    Your Body is Energy Vibrating at a Particular
    Frequency 80
    Only an Enlightened Master Can Open THE
    Ananda Gandha Chakra 81
    Ananda Gandha and the Seven Energy Bodies 81
    Ananda Gandha and the Five Koshas 83
    Ananda Gandha and the Four States
    of Consciousness 84
    The Time Shaft 85
    Discovering the Right Key 87
    Master Can Simply Pull You into
    Ananda Gandha 87
    The 21- Minute Cycle 88

Ananda Gandha Meditation 91

Shakti Dharana Meditation 95
    Meditation Instructions 95

Nithya Dhyaan 99
    Nithya Dhyaan Meditation Explained 100
        1. Chaotic Breathing 100
        2. Intense Humming 102
        3. *Chakra* Awareness 104
        4. Be Unclutched 104
        5. *Guru Puja* 108
    Benefits of Nithya Dhyaan * 110

Healing Testimonials (Part I) 112
Ananda Darshan 117

Healing Testimonials (Part II) 128

A Promise to Yourself - Healers' Oaths 133
    Why no To Drinking, Smoking or Eating
    Non-vegetarian Food After Healers' Initiation 133
    Oath 1 134
    Compassion for Each and Every one 135
    Drop Your Vengeance and Become Free 137
        The Healing Touch of Love 138
    Oath 2 139
    Oath 3 140
    Significance of the Homa Ritual 141
    Ananda Gandha Initiation 141

Healing Testimonials (Part III) 143

Spiritual Name 148
    What is in a Name? 148
    Significance of the Spiritual Name 148

Nithya Spiritual Healing 152
In Practice 152
    Healer's Chart 153
    Etiquette for Nithya Spiritual Healers 156

Healing Testimonials (Part IV) 159

Chakra Counseling 165
    Classification of Chakras 166
    Same Chakra Solution 167
    Complementary Chakra Solution 167
    Life Solution 167

Guidelines for Nithya Spiritual Healing 169

Surya Namaskar 173
    Benefits of Surya Namaskar 173
    Significance of Surya Namaskar Mantras 174
    Breathe In Suffering, Breathe Out Bliss 177
    Asana Sequence of Surya Namaskar 177
    Ashtanga Yoga - the Eightfold Path to Bliss for the Healer 181

Your Questions Answered 185

Healing Testimonials (Part V) 195

Nithya Spiritual Healing
   As a Service 200
    The Same Power of Healing of the
    Master is With The Healer 202
    Modes of Service 202
        Free Nithya Spiritual Healing Centers 202
        Free Nithya Spiritual Healing Camps 203
        Dhyanapeetam Healing Temples 204

Healing Testimonials (Part VI) 207

Healers' Meet - August 9, 2006 212
    Why Healers' Meet 212
    Why Ananda Gandha Meditation 212
    Three Categories of Healers 214
    Meditations to be Done by All Healers 215

Healing Products 217
    Rudraksha Mala 217
    Red Sandalwood Mala 218
    Nithyanandam Bracelet 219
    Kumkum (Vermilion mark) 219
    Vibhuti 220
    Yantras 220

Healers' Meet - December 30, 2006 223

Healing Testimonials (Part VII) 227

Living in *Ananda Gandha* 232
    Living in *Ananda Gandha* is Enlightenment 232
    Ananda Gandha - Connection to Cosmic
    Intelligence 232
    You are the Center of the Universe 233
    Our *Ananda Gandha* is an Extension of
    master's *Ananda Gandha* 234
    Research findings... 235
    DNA Phantom Effect 235
    Cloning Enlightenment 237

    Living 24 Hours in Ananda Gandha 237
    Annamaya Kosha Meditation technique 238
    Pranamaya Kosha Meditation 242
        The Pranic System 242
        Pranamaya Kosha Meditation technique 243
    Effect of Emotions on the Structure of DNA 245

Collective Consciousness 248
    Our Thoughts Affect the Very Structure
    of Water 251
    Natural Calamities and Collective Negativity 253
    Decide Your Destiny! 254

Appendix 256

Table of Figures

Figure 1: Physiological Effects of Fear   20

Figure 2: Macrocosm and Microcosm   21

Figure 3: Seven *Chakras* and their locations in the body   33

Figure 4: *Ananda Gandha* and the 7 *chakras*   80

Figure 5: Seven Energy Bodies and relation Between You, God and I   82

Figure 6: Five *Koshas* (Energy Sheaths)   83

Figure 7: Four States of Consciousness   84

Figure 8: Time Shaft   86

Figure 9: Chaotic Breathing   100

Figure 10: *Chin Mudra*   102

Figure 11: *Chakra* Awareness   104

Figure 12: *Guru Puja*   108

Figure 13: *Surya Namaskar Mantras*   176

Figure 14: *Rudraksha Mala*   217

Figure 15: Red Sandalwood *Mala*   218

Figure 16: *Nithyanandam* Bracelet   219

Figure 17: *Kumkum* and Paste   219

Figure 18: *Sri Chakra Yantras*   220

Heal The Universe

Chapter 1
Heal The Universe

Question:

1. In one of your research reports, I read that high blood pressure can become normal, and low blood pressure can also become normal through the same technique of Nithya Spiritual Healing. How is that possible?

That is a very nice question.

Medically, the medicine given for high blood pressure and low blood pressure are two different medicines.

Here, we are giving healing as medicine for both. If you see superficially, the healer does the same thing of placing his or her hands on the person receiving the healing. How does it heal two totally different problems? It seems difficult to understand. A person thinking and analyzing with the mind cannot logically understand.

Healing and meditation work at a level beyond the mind.

Nithya Spiritual Healing is healing through cosmic energy. This is different from energy as we knows in various forms such as electric energy. Cosmic energy is intelligence. Electric energy does not have its own intelligence. If you fix a bulb in a socket, the current will flow and the bulb will glow. If you put your hand in the electric socket, in the same way the current will flow, but it will give you an electric shock! Although energy is often compared to an electric current, this healing energy is not like that. It can never do anything wrong, because **cosmic energy has its own independent intelligence**.

Whether it is high blood pressure or low blood pressure, it is the same healing energy, which helps the body in its healing. Nithya Spiritual Healing is actually a meditation.

To explain how healing and meditation really work, we need to understand ourselves in relation to the five elements which constitute every single thing on planet earth: earth, water, fire, air and space. Another important thing we need to realize is:

The body *(pindaanda)* is the *cmicrocosmic* representation of the *macrocosmic* universe *(brahmaanda)*. Both are made up of these five elements.

Ayurveda and *Siddha* are two beautiful traditional systems of medicine that embody this truth. They are based on the principle of the *panchabhutas* (five elements) and the three *doshas* (attributes). The three attributes are *vatha* which is based on the air element, *pitha* based on the fire element and *kapha* based on the water element. In these systems, the definition of health itself is having these three attributes in balance, in harmony with each other. The *siddha* system of medicine defines the right proportion of *vatha, pitha and kapha* at 1: 0.5 : 0.25 for a healthy body-mind system. When this balance is disturbed due to wrong food habits, unhealthy lifestyle, etc, 'disease' happens and the relevant medicine has to be given to restore the balance.

The complex system of the human body is working so beautifully and seemingly effortlessly. Similarly, the universe is balancing so amazingly with billions of galaxies, stars, planets, black holes, comets and so many other heavenly bodies. If you look at it, there seems to be a beautiful order even though no obvious system is monitoring the motion of the galaxies!

There are so many theories on how the universe is balancing and how the body is working. To explain it simply, the five elements are continuously balancing, whether inside the body or outside in the universe.

If there is a fire and we pour water on it, immediately the fire subsides. That is the nature of the relation between fire and water. When fire and water come together, the heat of the fire is reduced by the coolness of the water.

In the same manner as a fire outside is put down by water, so also there is a fire inside our body. You may have heard of the digestive fire *(jataraagni)* inside our body. Similarly, there are other different types of fires or 'fevers' that happen in the body.

Sixty four different types of fevers exist in our body.

In our body, a kind of fever exists continuously. In our *vedic* scriptures, our *rishis* (sages) classify sixty four fevers.

For example, your anger is a fever. When you get angry, if you are sensitive, you can feel a burning sensation in the eye. When you feel sexual arousal, the whole body feels the heat.

When you go through an emotion, without your knowledge, the temperature of the body increases or decreases. Please understand: the heat getting reduced is also fever.

Let us explain this fever in medical terms. Take fear, for example. Fear is an emotion which is triggered by the mind in the form of a fearful thought. The fear thought can be created by any means, like when seeing a snake or when hearing a threatening word.

Physiologically, any thought triggers the relevant hormones in the blood stream. In the case of the fear thought, it touches the adrenaline gland. This releases the adrenaline hormone.

The adrenaline hormone creates the 'fight or flight' reaction. You either fight with the fear, or run away in flight.

Whether it is a 'fight' reaction or a 'flight' reaction, the body needs extra energy to execute the required action. You need the support of the chemicals in the body. The hormones have to be released into the blood stream. The muscles which are normally relaxed have to become tense. The supply of oxygen and glucose to the brain and muscles has to be increased, while suppressing the non-emergency functions like digestion.

An important thing we need to understand is that the stress hormones like adrenaline suppress the immune system. Naturally, when the immune system is suppressed, your body is more prone to falling ill.

In the olden days, this stress reaction would happen for survival purposes. It was not a regular occurrence like it has become today. Today, stress has become a part of every moment of our lives. The natural effect of stress is that the immune system gets suppressed. The hormones that were meant to be released once in a while and get dissipated naturally are now present in the system continuously. The immune system is constantly suppressed.

If the emotional fever comes once in a while to save us from danger, it is ok. But when it happens continuously, like the fear of a student with the teacher or anger of the employee with the boss, the hormones are released again and again and the body gets too much heat. Every cell burns with that emotion.

In the outside world, when there is a fire, you put water and it cools down. In the body, the water element is blood. The blood travels and supplies the hormones. Also, it cleans the area and reduces the temperature of the area.

The continuous 'fear strokes' and emotional upsets and anger result in the need for increased blood supply.

For a normal person the heart beats at the average rate of 72 times per minute. But to manage a stressful situation, the 72 heartbeats per minute can go up to 90 heartbeats per minute or beyond. To manage the different fevers, pumping 80 or 90 times per minute becomes a normal function for the heart, instead of the emergency function it was meant to be. So, the average heart rate goes up from 72 heartbeats per minute to 90 heartbeats per minute. That is why the blood pressure increases.

If you are a high blood pressure patient, to reduce blood pressure medically, you take a tablet. The same tablet if taken by a low blood pressure patient will lower the blood pressure further in him. For a low blood pressure patient the tablet needed is different - one that will increase the blood pressure. Medicine touches only the symptom of the problem exhibited by the body and not the real source of the problem.

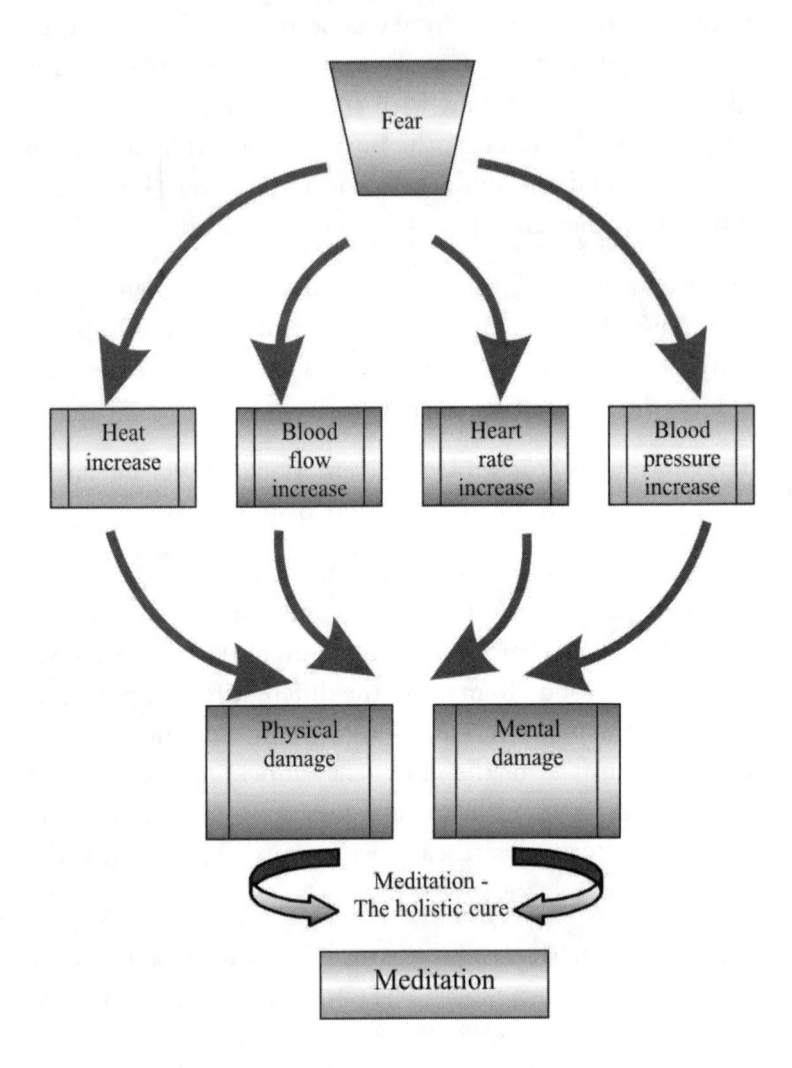

Figure 1: Physiological Effects of Fear

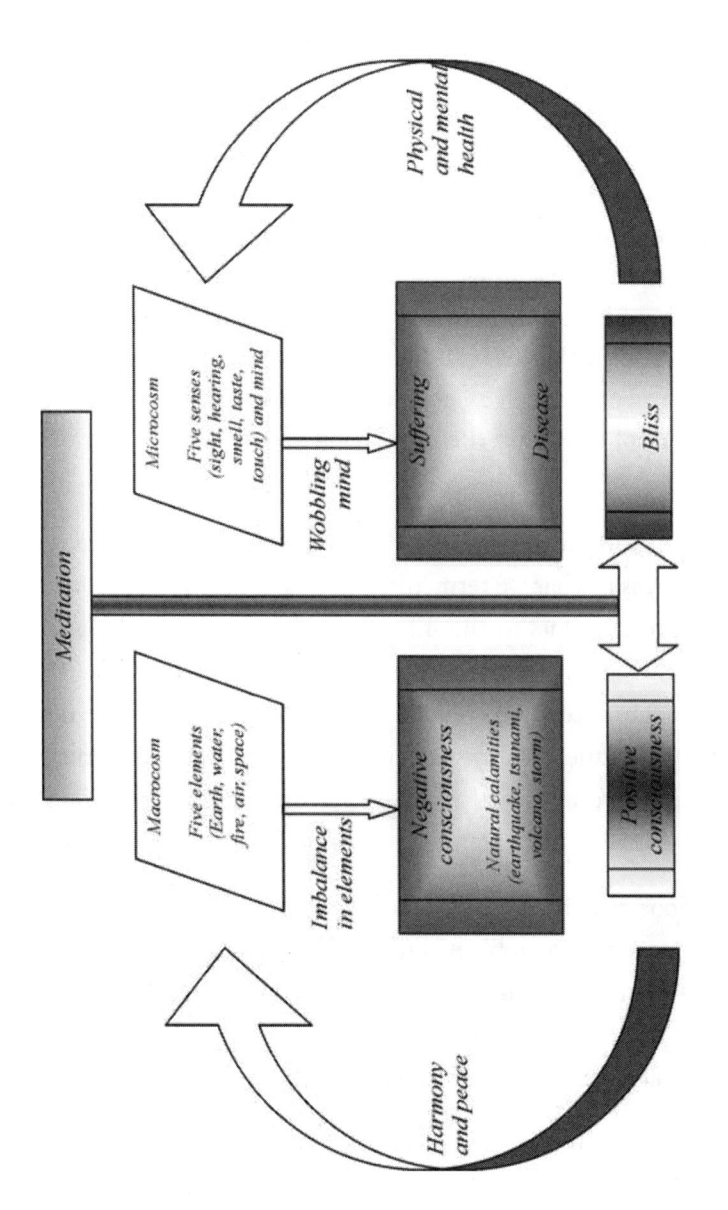

Figure 2: Macrocosm and Microcosm

Abnormal blood pressure levels are not the root problem. The mind that is creating the disease is the real problem.

Various natural calamities happen in the universe because of the imbalance of the five elements. For example, today we are indiscriminately boring into the earth, whether for quarrying or digging for oil or water etc. This creates a vacuum in the earth. To support the vacuum, the earth has to readjust itself to maintain the balance of the five elements. The adjustments result in earthquakes that we call 'natural calamities'. Actually it is an adjustment of the five elements in the macrocosm in response to our act of changing the proportion and balance of the five elements.

So also in the microcosm, the body, various natural calamities happen; this is what we term 'disease'. Disease is the adjustment of the five elements in the microcosm. The natural calamities in the microcosm, whether it is a tumor, cancer or AIDS for example, are actually the effects of our actions. But we are not able to realize this, because we do so many of our actions without awareness. We term the effect of our unconscious living and choices made in unawareness as 'disease'.

You cannot treat the effect. You can only address the cause. Treating the disease as only a problem of the body is treating the effect. Can you suppress a tsunami by using a big blowing machine? The tsunami will just take a different course. If there is a block in one area, it will manifest in a different area.

We are trying to fix the hardware, the body, when it is the software, the mind, that is issuing the wrong instructions! The software is corrupted; so it is continuously giving the wrong instructions. The mental setup is the root cause of the problem and the diseases and imbalances in our body-mind are just the manifestations of our habit of wrong thinking.

Enlightened masters can replace the corrupt software by positive software. The negative software can be neutralized.

Just by positive thinking we cannot become enlightened.

We have to transcend both the 'good' and the 'bad' thinking.

There is no difference between good and bad garbage. In the same way, if you look deeply you will see that there is nothing called 'positive thinking' and 'negative thinking'. It is all 'thinking'.

We have to cross thinking itself. The thoughts per second (TPS) expressing in our system have to reduce. When the TPS is reduced, the heart rate is reduced. When the heart rate is reduced, the blood flow reduces. When we provide a negative stimulus (one that reduces the heart rate), the heart rate reduces. This negative stimulus can also be provided by medication. This has no effect on the underlying cause of the 'fever', the mind. Reducing the thoughts per second (TPS) can only be achieved with meditation.

Because the impulse is reduced, the stimulus does not go to the body. The effect is that the increased heart rate drops from 90 beats per minute to the normal rate of 72 beats per minute. Because the stimulus itself is stopped, the root cause of the problem is eliminated.

Similarly, for a person with low blood pressure, the heart rate increases gradually from 60 beats per minute to the normal rate of 72 beats per minute.

Meditation, especially Nithya Dhyaan (explained later in the book), if done consistently for 48 days, will lower the TPS and normalize both high and low blood pressure.

When the TPS reduces, the mind comes to a steady state and thoughts do not arise. The heart rate returns to normal, which results in vibrant health.

But please be very clear that 'meditation as a medicine' is just a secondary use of meditation. Restoring good health is just one of the side-benefits of meditation. Using meditation as a master tool for self-transformation to realize who we really are is the ultimate and intended use of meditation techniques.

Question:

2. How do depression and stress get resolved with meditation?

Your question is a very common question coming from the masses as to whether meditation will get us out of depression.

Please be clear: meditation will move you from depression to expression and thus straightaway get rid of depression.

We can classify our body-mind-spirit system in different ways. One such classification is through the system of *koshas*. The *annamaya kosha* is related to the physical body, which is the body we can see, touch and feel. The *pranamaya kosha* is related to the breath, which is directly and deeply related to our desires. The *manomaya kosha* is related to our mental thoughts. The *vijnanamaya kosha* is related to all our feelings and emotions. The *anandamaya kosha* is related to the bliss in us - our true nature.

In the five *koshas*, depression is in the outermost layer, the *annamaya kosha* or physical layer. Meditation works from the innermost layer, the *anandamaya kosha* or bliss layer.

Depression is *not* a psychological problem.
It is *not* a mental problem, it is a *physical* problem.

When the mind works too actively, the body is not able to handle it and depression is the result of that overload on the body.

Physiologically, the depression comes from the depression chemicals released inside your system. When you feel depressed, if you take a little coffee, you come out of the depression because the caffeine in the coffee stimulates you. Similarly, when you smoke, the nicotine stimulates you. The chemicals released by coffee or tobacco in your body counter the effect of the depression chemicals in your body and that is why you get a 'high'.

However, this kind of chemical support to get out of depression is like using acid to clean a car! To clean a car, we cannot use acid as we would use to clean a sink. In the case of our body-mind, to come out of depression we try similar techniques like taking intoxicants or stimulants that are self-damaging.

The depression you feel is a physical phenomenon resulting from the chemicals released in your body. That is why a good aroma can get you out of depression, because it will release the opposite chemicals that will counter the depression chemicals.

With meditation, there is a higher intelligence working on the body, beyond the mind that is creating the problem.

Meditation releases the bliss chemicals that are not only an antidote for depression but which by their very nature take you beyond both the feelings of depression and 'the high'.

Meditation not only supports the system with positive energy; it supports with intelligent consciousness.

The replacement is total. It is like replacing poison with nectar. The negative energy is replaced with consciousness. Healing replaces the negative energy with consciousness. Just like when a light brought into a room makes the darkness disappear; in the same way, when you bring meditation into your life, stress and depression are removed as side effects of the process.

When energy passes through and overflows from the healer, the recipient receives it. Stress is removed since the intelligent energy floods the body-mind. The healer also benefits from this extra energy and any stress in the healer's system is removed.

The energy restores the intelligence to the body, consciousness to the mind and rich vibrancy to life.

Because it is restoring what you already have within you at your core, but have forgotten, it just brings you back in touch with your true nature of bliss which can never be lost. That is why healing and meditation result in permanent effects.

It rejuvenates the whole being and wherever there is imbalance, by its very intelligence, the imbalance is corrected and disease does not exist anymore. The person is transformed by the healing energy and experiences health, energy and enthusiasm.

Introduction to Healing

Chapter 2
Introduction to Healing

What is Healing?

> Pythagoras (Greek Scientist & Mathematician) said that the most divine art was that of healing. And if the healing art is most divine, it must occupy itself with the soul as well as with the body; for no creature can be sound so long as the higher part in it is sickly.
>
> - Apollonius of Tyana (A Greek Philosopher)

Buddha, an enlightened master gives a beautiful explanation or definition for the word 'healing'. He says healing is our way of expressing our compassion, expressing our care towards somebody to help restore his health to him.

Healing is nothing but helping a person restore his physical, mental and emotional well-being. At any level healing can happen. We can help somebody restore his physical well-being and vibrancy. We can help somebody restore his mental well-being. We can help somebody restore his emotional well-being and balance. At whatever level we help, that is healing.

According to me, allowing 'Him' to work on us is healing. When I say Him, I mean the divine personality, the divine energy. We may call Him by various names, but allowing Him to work on us is healing.

Arogya or Good Health

Good health is not just an absence of disease, it is a positive *well-being-ness*. We are not just humans who are meant to fall sick and get cured. We are an abode of bliss. We were created to feel this bliss continuously inside us and to float with blissful lightness at the Being level. This is what is called *arogya* or good health.

We are ever ready to spend our time, money and energy curing ourselves of some ailment or discomfort. Or we believe that such problems are an unavoidable part of living. We have become so caught up in the cycle of disease and cure that we see disease as an inevitable disaster that has a cure in the outer world. We do not know the root cause of all disease and imbalance.

Actually, every ailment or disease has got its root in the mind. For example, continuous worrying leads to stomach ulcers. Every emotion of ours causes a disturbance in the energy level in us, in our system, which in turn manifests itself at the physical level as disease.

Healing at the Physical, Mental and Emotional Levels

There are so many levels of healing. Healing does not mean healing only our physical illness or healing our pain. Healing means experiencing a feeling of well-being. If we can say a few courteous words to others which makes them feel comfortable and joyful, even that has a healing effect.

Emotional Healing

An experiment was conducted in The Ohio University in the 1970s to study heart disease. Rabbits were fed a high cholesterol diet to create blockage of their arteries. All the rabbit groups showed consistent results except one; strangely this group showed 60 percent fewer symptoms than the rest of the rabbit groups.

It was discovered that the student who was in charge of feeding this group of rabbits was in the habit of fondling and petting them. He used to hold each rabbit lovingly for a few minutes each day before feeding them. It was amazing that this alone seemed to enable the animals to overcome the natural results of a toxic diet.

When experiments were repeated with one group treated neutrally and the other group lovingly, the same results were reproduced.

We underestimate the power of our thoughts and emotions. They have a very deep impact on our mind and body.

History of Healing

The first thing that man asks for is always physical and mental health. With any religion or master, the first utility or gain that man looks for is 'good health'. Only when given this guarantee does he look further into fulfilling his deeper longings. Only then does he move on towards meditation, enlightenment, etc.

From time immemorial, all religions and all masters have demonstrated healing powers.

Introduction to Healing

In fact, no master is accepted as a master if he cannot restore health in people in some form or the other. Healing has become a measure of a master's identity.

There are various instances of masters healing the world. Krishna, an enlightened master healing Kubja, the hunchback, is described in the Srimad Bhagavatam (ancient Hindu epic composed by the seer Veda Vyasa). Ahalya, who was so filled with guilt that she had turned to stone, was healed by Rama's (an incarnation of the Hindu God – Vishnu) touch. There are various instances in the Bible about Jesus Christ healing the sick.

Man needs a tangible way by which he can differentiate between an ordinary person and a super-conscious energy. Invariably the method to differentiate is by way of the healing powers exhibited by the person.

Even in tribal villages, the religion followed will have healing as its core. There are many stories that we hear about healing. A famous story goes like this: A man sits in a corner with ragged clothes and barely any belongings. When people go near him, he throws stones at them and they get miraculously healed of life-long ailments. People immediately recognize him as a master. They therefore never disturb him in his place. If it had not been for the healing, he would have been treated as nothing short of a beggar. But because of the healing effect of his energy, the beggar becomes a *Mahatma* or God.

- A scientist is a person who creates a formula to reproduce the same things that he discovered in the outer world so that others can also understand.

- A *rishi* is a person who creates a formula to reproduce the same experience that happened in him in the inner world so that it happens spontaneously in others.

- An *avatar* (incarnation) is a being who can simply **put** other people into the same experience that he had, without even giving a formula!

PATANJALI'S SYSTEM OF HEALING

There are various levels of healing. Patanjali, the father of the Yoga system, was the first 'inner scientist' to actually map the route to the Truth in the inner world. He developed a system of enlightenment. Until then, enlightenment was not a science. Step by step he created the Patanjali Yoga Sutras - the Ashtanga Yoga.

There are thousands of great masters, *rishis* and mystics who were healers. Almost all the spiritual masters expressed their energy with the ability to heal others. There was and is no master, mystic or *rishi* whose life is not associated with at least one or two healing miracles.

Human beings have always gone to masters to get healed, especially in the East.

There are thousands and thousands of records and testimonials to show that that there is something called healing. Whether at the physical, mental, emotional, psychological or being level, healing continues to happen by so many masters in so many ways.

Introduction to Healing

Let us see the healing system created by the great master Patanjali.

CHAKRAS - SUBTLE, POWERFUL ENERGY CENTERS

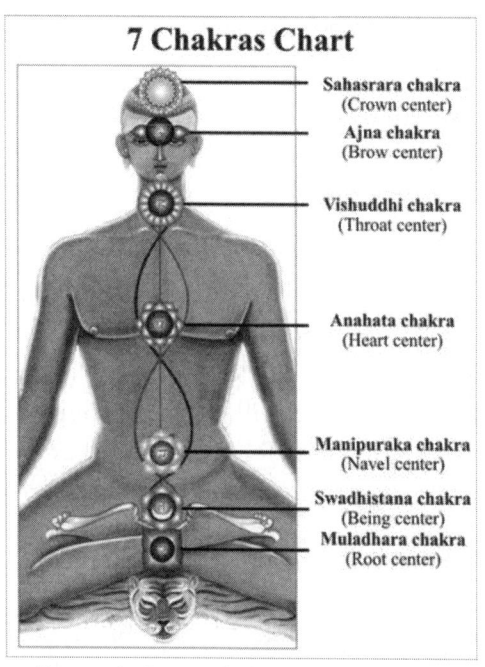

Figure 3: Seven chakras & their location in the body

- Sahasrara chakra (Crown center)
- Ajna chakra (Brow center)
- Vishuddhi chakra (Throat center)
- Anahata chakra (Heart center)
- Manipuraka chakra (Navel center)
- Swadhistana chakra (Being center)
- Muladhara chakra (Root center)

According to Patanjali, there are seven *chakras* or subtle energy centers in our body.

These seven energy centers are the masters of our physical, mental, emotional, psychological, intellectual and being level activities and manage all of the activities arising from these areas within us.

The metaphysical locations of the *chakras* can be roughly associated with seven major glands in our physical bodies. *Chakras* are the energy centers which make the corresponding physical glands work.

Proof of *Chakras* through Kirlian Photography

We may wonder: what proof is there that *chakras* do exist? The concept of energy centers within the human system may have been dismissed even a few decades ago for the simple reason that there was no tangible proof of its existence. In recent times, Kirlian photography and other techniques have demonstrated that there are energy fields surrounding us.

This new kind of photography called Kirlian photography was made popular in Russia. With X-rays we can find out about bone fracture or tuberculosis. So also with Kirlian photography, we can see the energy field around a person. The beauty is that the energy field will show the signs of impending physical changes much before these changes are reflected in the physical body.

With Kirlian photography, we can photograph the aura body of every single individual. 'Aura' means the subtle light, which is continuously emitted by one's body. By photographing that light, Kirlian photographers are able to diagnose any disease, which is going to occur in a person. They say that upto six months prior to the disease actually manifesting itself physically, they are able to diagnose it through the science of Kirlian photography.

Ill health can be prevented even before a person has any idea that he is about to fall sick. Through Kirlian photography, a person can observe energy imbalances and determine what aspect of the body-mind will be adversely affected.

With this system we can see the energy fields of the *chakras*. It has been shown that if a person is depressed and dull, the *chakras* shrink to the size of a coat-button. If the person is joyful, blissful and ecstatic, the energy field of the *chakras* expands and becomes the size of a car wheel. Just the change of mood from dullness to joy causes our energy field to expand to a size almost sixty to seventy times greater than when it is in a contracted state.

Chakras and Emotions

There is extensive research recorded by various scientists studying the efficacy of various healing techniques. They all acknowledge that the mind has a major impact on the body.

Each and every one of our *chakras* is related to some emotion in us. For example, love is related to the anahata chakra, the heart center. You can see in many of the world's languages, the words 'heart' and 'love' are synonymous. It is not that God created all the languages on one day and made pronunciation packages and dropped them! It is a strange 'coincidence' that in all the languages 'heart' and 'love' are synonymous.

When, after a very long time you see one of your childhood friends with whom you have cherished loving memories. The moment you see him or her, you can feel something flowing from your heart region: that is what we call love which is related to the *anahata chakra*.

In the same way, the navel *chakra* is related to worry. If you receive some news that is shocking which you are not able to 'digest', the first blow will be to your stomach and you will land up with a stomach upset. The stomach is very closely associated with worry.

Each and every emotion is related to one of your *chakras* or energy centers. If that emotion is used properly, the *chakra* functions well. If the emotion is abused, the *chakra* gets blocked.

MAN BY NATURE IS BLISS

Rishis have declared that the very nature of man is bliss. It is our nature to experience bliss, even though most often we don't realize it. Children are always in bliss but progressively lose it as they grow up. Bliss is continuously happening in us, yet we do not experience it at all. Why? We are constantly stopping the flow of energy that results in bliss. We stop the 'eternal fountain of bliss' through all our negative emotions which are not our true nature and which actually have no solid existence. This in turn causes blockages in our *chakras*.

Several negative factors like childhood traumas, cultural conditioning, restrictive or exhausting habits, physical and emotional injuries, or even just lack of healthy attention when you are craving for it, all contribute to the blockages in the energy flow through the *chakras*.

For each perceived difficulty in our lives, we develop a coping strategy. When the difficulties persist, these coping strategies become chronic patterns, anchored in the body as defence structures. And this in turn prevents the free flow of energy in our system, in our being. So we stagnate and become a closed system in which the *chakras* are blocked. It is important to recognize the blocks we carry, find ways to understand their source and meaning and develop ways to heal them.

It is only when our *chakras* are blocked that disease sets in. When our body and mind are at ease with each other, we always feel easiness, the *easeness* in us. When our body and mind are not at ease with each other, we feel the *dis-easeness*, the disease.

THE POWER OF THOUGHT

Most of the diseases are psychosomatic. They originate from the mind and are then expressed in the body. The root is the mind, not the body.

Actually the mind and body are two aspects of the same phenomenon; mind and body are not two different things. That is why the body is a psychosomatic phenomenon.

Mind is the subtlest part of the body, and the body is the grossest part of the mind.

Both the body and mind affect each other. They function on parallel tracks. When we suppress something in the mind, the body will begin a suppressing path. If the mind releases everything the body also releases everything.

The Brihadaranya Upanishad states, 'As our thoughts are, so is our will; as our will is, so is our action; as our action is, so is our destiny.'

Cosmic energy is linked to individual energy through the *chakras*. The separation we experience is only our illusion. Just like the water in a harbor is connected to the water of the ocean, so too the energy we have flowing through us is connected to the inexhaustible reservoir of cosmic energy. It is possible for us to tap into that inexhaustible cosmic energy. The inner scientists of the Eastern *vedic* traditions have done so for thousands of years and continue to do so today. Instead of living in a shackled compartment of depleted energy we can live in vibrant, continuous energetic health and bliss.

When the *chakras* in our body are disturbed because of the suppression in the mind, then we become diseased. There are several techniques to release these blocks which results in a healthy body. When the body is healthy we see tremendous new energies flowing, new dimensions revealing themselves, new doors suddenly opening up to new possibilities of creative, intelligent expression in our lives.

It is the mind that prevents the body from being used as an instrument to experience the bliss in ourselves. But most of us feel that our body is the enemy and that our senses are destroying us. We are taught from childhood that the body is our enemy and we have to control it. When we allow our body's natural intelligence to function, we don't have to control it. When we are in tune with that natural intelligence, we make choices that support our health rather than diminish it. We then develop a deep, loving and beautiful relationship with the body.

BODY INTELLIGENCE

Our bodies have a natural intelligence of their own. We don't have to be afraid of our body or control and suppress it in the ways that we have been taught.

Introduction to Healing

CONTROL OF THE SENSES IS NOT NEEDED

Suppose you go to a restaurant and are tempted by the smell of French fries being made, you resist the temptation and are angry with yourself for craving for junk food. If you look deeply though, you will see that the temptation is not from your sense of taste but from your mind. You may have seen advertisements everywhere and they would have made an impact on your mind without even your knowledge and awareness. Somehow or the other you have the idea that eating French fries will make you happy and you will enjoy it.

Sometime in the past you may have eaten French fries driven by this craving from the unconscious mind. But you might have eaten them feeling guilty for eating junk food. Or your mind was distracted with other thoughts as you ate. So your desire was not 'fulfilled' even though your stomach was filled. It is likely that you never ate even one serving of French fries with full awareness and intensity; so the craving for them was never fully satisfied. Now that unfulfilled desire from the mind rises again when you smell the French fries.

You see, it is the mind that is involved in this whole game, not the body.

Someone asked me, 'Don't we have to control the senses?' It is our senses, not the body, that are responsible for our attachments and aversions. But we don't know how to differentiate between the body and the senses. The only thing we know clearly is the gross body, so we start controlling it.

Gradually with a lot of practice, you can succeed in controlling your senses and suppressing them. You only become insensitive by doing this. You could end up losing all your sensitivity and your joy of life without attaining real transformation.

Instead, enter into a relationship of deep love and respect with your body and with the world. Drop all negativity, all hostility, and all ideas of controlling the body. The truth is, whatever is controlled will express itself in some other way. It will refuse to be controlled! We just have to drop the negativity and see how our life changes.

A real incident:

Once a young man came to me and asked me to help him stop smoking. I asked him how he picked up the habit in the first place. He said that once he had gone out with a group of friends who were all smokers. He happened to meet his father on the road that day. Seeing him in the group, his father assumed that he too had been smoking. When he returned home, his father yelled at him, refusing to believe that his son had not been smoking. The next day, the boy says, he smoked a whole pack of cigarettes just to spite his father! In this way he gradually got addicted.

When he asked me how to drop it, I told him, 'Don't drop it. Go ahead and smoke. But don't do it to prove anything to anybody. Don't do it to spite your father. And don't imagine that you have become mature and independent by smoking. Every time you pick up a cigarette, do it silently. Be conscious of why you are smoking. You will realize on your own.'

After just a few days the boy returned to me. He said, 'Swamiji, I am not able to smoke anymore! Doing it consciously, I realized that I was not smoking for the sake of smoking. Smoking is not that important to me.' Then he added something which made me very

Introduction to Healing

happy. He said, 'Swamiji, I realize now that I have been abusing my body all these days, by pushing smoke into my system!'

When we become conscious of what we are doing, many things drop by themselves. This is the only permanent solution.

Of course, it may take a few days to awaken the natural intelligence. The patience to wait till then is what is called *tapasya*, penance. It is important that in this period of *tapasya*, you don't give up and fall back on second-rate intelligence that you have picked up from the moral codes set up by society. Have trust in your body.

We always live in deep fear of our bodies. We feel as if we are sitting on a live volcano. The moment we sense a cold or fever coming up, the day we have the slightest headache, we reach out for a pill. It has become totally acceptable for us to swallow pills for any and all symptoms. Most of our common ailments can be easily handled with a little care. But we don't credit our body with the power to heal itself. When our body can digest food, pump blood, mend broken bones and perform a thousand other complicated tasks without our conscious help or assistance from outside, can't it take care of a fever or a headache?

Allow your body to function according to its own intelligence. You will see for yourself how much wisdom your body has. In order to experience this natural body intelligence we need to drop our doubt. We must have the courage to experiment and the trust to test this in our life. Then we will find there is tremendous body intelligence available to us and there is no need to control the body at all.

Intelligence Down to the Cellular Level

Another amazing, probably shocking revelation to most of us is that our intelligence and awareness do not exist only in our brain. We think that we are handling the body from the brain. It has long been proven through scientific research that the brain controls respiration, digestion, blood circulation, etc. The nervous system controls the whole body's neural activities. To date, we have believed that the brain, like the nucleus in a cell, controls the whole body and its activities.

However, cutting-edge research has given rise to a new field called epigenetics. Dr. Bruce Lipton, an eminent biologist, has been doing research in this field of epigenetics for over 10 years. In his book, 'Biology of Belief', he states that our brain does *not* control our body. intelligence is actually present in every cell, in fact in its cellular membrane. In the same way that the intelligence and awareness exists in the cell membrane of a cell, the intelligence and awareness of the body exists in the aura - the energy field that extends beyond the body.

> ### The Power of Self-contradiction
>
> An experiment was conducted where a cell was put in a dish. A rich nutrient was placed close to it. The cell started moving towards this rich nutrient. Then a poisonous substance was put in another dish and the cell was put in that dish next to the poisonous substance. The cell, instead of moving towards it, started moving in the opposite direction.
>
> Then both the nutrient and poisonous substance were put in the same dish with the cell in the center. Surprisingly, the cell did not move. When it was put in a good medium, the cell moved towards it. When it was put in a poisonous

medium, the cell moved away from it. But when both the nutrient and poison were placed next to it, the cell intelligence was confused and could not respond. This shows how we also get confused with 'self-contradictory' thoughts in our life.

For example, when you tell yourself, 'I want to quit smoking', you are giving equal power to the word 'smoking' and to your desired goal, 'quit'. Essentially, both the words 'quit' and 'smoking' are being entertained, which leads to a mutually canceling situation. That is why you are not able to get out of the problem.

MATTER-ENERGY EQUIVALENCE - THE BASIS OF ENERGY HEALING

Today, science also accepts that matter and energy are equivalent. Einstein's equation $E=mc^2$ shows the equivalence of matter and energy.

Thousands of years back, our *Upanishads* (Ancient texts from *vedic* tradition) declared this Truth. The first line of the first *Upanishad*, the Isavasya Upanishad says, *'Isa vasyam idam sarvam'* - whatever exists is energy. There is no difference between matter and energy. Solid energy is matter; subtle matter is energy. Matter and energy are one and the same.

Whatever you label as matter is nothing but energy. Whatever you call energy is nothing but matter. Whatever exists is energy.

From this scientific and spiritual declaration we can now draw the conclusion that if matter can be given to somebody else, why can't energy be shared? If I can hand you a watch, why can't I give you energy also? All that is needed is knowing the proper technique or method of giving it. In order to give you a watch, I have to pick it up, move it through space and hand it to you. In the same way, energy has to be channeled properly for it to reach its intended destination. If a person knows the right technique of channeling and giving energy, it can be shared. If you know the technique, you know the science and it is no longer a miracle.

What kind of things do we consider to be miracles? Let us say there is a bell on the table next to me. If I take it in my hand, will you call it a miracle? No. But if one moment the same bell just jumps into my hand, you would call it a miracle, is it not? Actually, in the first case I move the bell physically while in the second case I move it with my mental power, that's all. I disintegrate the bell, converting the matter to energy, then integrate it back in my hand, thereby converting energy to matter, that's all. But because you don't know this technique, you think it is a miracle. Because this is not commonly understood it is 'supernatural.'

The science of giving the energy to a person who is sick or in need of energy is what we call healing. The energy can be given to any *chakra*, any energy center that needs it, and the energy center responds to it.

If we ourselves can get the right technique and make enough time to use the right technique, we can remove the blockages, come out of disease and restore the *chakra* to its energy balance. There are various reasons why we are all not able to do this at all times. Some of us may not know the right technique or make enough time to meditate. Because of poor health we may not have enough energy for meditation and spiritual practices. In such cases, someone who is a meditator can meditate and pass the energy to the energy centers of the person who is in disease. This is the essence of the science of energy healing.

Apart from the intellectual explanation of healing, we have thousands of records, medical data and substantiation along with research reports, including those done in our ashram to prove the science of Nithya Spiritual Healing. We have studied and proven how energy is given, how and where the energy works in the system and how it heals the disease.

WHO CAN GIVE ENERGY? ONE WHO HAS REALIZED HE IS ENERGY

Who can give energy? The man who has realized that he is energy, the one who has experienced himself as something beyond the body and mind, is the only one who is authorized or qualified to give energy. Naturally you start radiating and expressing the energy that has become your experience. When you experience that you are something beyond the body and mind, only then can you radiate that inexhaustible energy. Until then you cannot radiate energy.

Whether you understand or not, whether you experience or not, whether you believe it or not, you are energy. The person who realizes it is the one who is qualified to share his energy.

People ask me, '*Swamiji*, do you chant any *mantra* when you heal? Please teach us, we will also do the same.'

I tell you, there is no other secret. I don't chant any mantra. When I touch, I just become the touch, that's all. My whole being touches, my whole being feels the energy. Your being is nothing but energy. Whether you believe it or not, your being is energy. If your being is not energy, how will you be alive?

Touch totally, that's all. It is the totality that heals; totality is always energy.

Who Can Receive Energy?
The Person with an Open Heart and Mind

Who can receive energy? Anybody who is in need can receive energy. There are a few tips that can be given to receive the energy in a beautiful way. People who are basically open-hearted, with an open mind, receive energy more easily and more quickly.

Many people ask me, '*Swamiji*, should we have faith to get healed?'

I tell them there is no need to have faith. To know the apple is tasty you don't need to believe, just have a bite; that's all. To know the sun is rising in the east you don't need to believe it. Just open your eyes and see. There is no need to blindly believe. To receive healing you don't need to have faith. You need to have only one thing: an open mind.

A small story:

One full moon night, an enlightened master was sitting outdoors and enjoying the beautiful scene: the night sky, the stars, and the cool breeze. In a nearby hut, he heard a man complaining bitterly about the miseries of life. So he went and called the man saying, 'Come out and enjoy this starry night, this full moon!'

Introduction to Healing

The man refused to believe that there was anything beautiful in his life. He said, 'No! I don't trust your words. First show me the moon, the stars; prove to me that they are beautiful and then I'll come out!'

The master replied, 'Just come out and you can see for yourself!'

But the man refused. Before even coming out, he wanted proof. How can you see unless you come out?

After a minute, the master suddenly started shouting, 'Your hut is on fire! Your hut is on fire!' Immediately, the man came rushing out of the hut.

Then suddenly, seeing the moonlit night and starry sky, he became lost in the beauty. He totally forgot that his house was supposed to be on fire. He exclaimed, 'Oh, it is so beautiful! When you told me I didn't believe you; but now I understand.'

Then suddenly he remembered, 'You told me that my hut was on fire. You lied to me!'

'Yes', said the master, 'I had to tell that lie to bring you out of your hut!'

When I say people with open minds, most people, especially those who live only based on logic, get the wrong idea that I mean people who trust anything.

All our colleges and universities help us sharpen our logic. But they are not able to help develop one of the major dimensions of human beings, their emotions. They help us sharpen our intellectual and logical thinking, but they have not done anything to help us grow emotionally. Because we have not grown emotionally, we have not experienced emotional intelligence, the emotional existence of our being.

We lack one major dimension of our lives. If a man is born without eyes, can you explain to that person what he is missing? No! You cannot explain to him what he is missing in his life. In the same way, the man who has never experienced the emotional aspect of himself, the man who has never trusted something, can never understand what it means to have a deep trust. He will not know directly what it means to have deep emotional intelligence, what it means to have a deep open heart.

Intellectual Growth Coupled with Emotional Growth

There is a beautiful saying in the Mahabharata: we all have three *balas* (strengths). One is physical strength, another is mental strength and the third is spiritual strength. Physical strength means physical health, physical well-being or physical power. The second is mental strength or intellectual power. The third is spiritual strength which is love and compassion.

If a man has only physical strength without spiritual strength, he will become a rogue, a rowdy, a criminal. If a man has only mental or intellectual strength without spiritual strength, he will only become a cunning person; he will not do any good. Only when you are endowed with spiritual strength, will the other two strengths, physical and mental, become useful for humanity. Somehow we miss spiritual strength, the emotional

Introduction to Healing

being, which is the reason that scientific advances have often been turned towards destructive uses.

Today we have atomic weapons on this planet earth which can burn the planet not once or twice, but seven hundred times over! All the countries have piled up atomic weapons that can burn planet earth seven hundred times. What is the reason? It is the right knowledge in the hands of the wrong persons. This is what happens when *shakti* (power) works without *buddhi* (intelligence). It is the surest way to destroy humanity.

Intellectual growth without emotional growth leads only to more and more danger. We all have worked towards intellectual growth, but have forgotten the emotional dimension.

Our *rishis*, our mystics, have worked on the development of the emotional dimension in humans. That is why every village in India has a big temple that is bigger than even the school or any other facility of the village. The temple is the primary thing for any village or settlement to be created. All other things are secondary. This is because our masters worked continuously to develop the emotional dimension of a human being. They knew that the development of emotions is the basic necessity for holistic growth and development. Once a man is developed in the emotional level, he will have everything; his life will be just heaven.

Some people ask me, 'In India our ancestors wasted all our energy building temples. Every village has got so many big temples. What is the need for having such big temples? See the other countries; they have all built big universities and scientific research centers. They have all built beautiful infrastructure - roads and bridges and all the possibilities for their economic growth. But our *rishis*, our masters, built only temples.'

I told them, 'Fools, you do not understand the greatness of our *rishis* and mystics. You say they wasted their energy in the temples but you do not realize that these temples are the basis of our emotional development. Because of these temples, our country is out of psychological disorders and diseases. Such a big country like India has only one percent of the population taking any medicine for mental disorders or diseases related to the mind.'

But in developed countries, we know the ratio. In some countries, out of three people, two are depression patients who are taking medicines for psychological problems. People are very proud to say, 'If I don't take my pills I cannot live!'

It is emotional development that gives a holistic growth to your personality. If you are whole, you are holy.

Sarada Devi, wife of Ramakrishna Paramahamsa (an enlightened master from West Bengal, India, who worshipped Goddess Kali), says beautifully, 'Live with deep trust, live with deep faith, live with deep love.' Of course when you love there is every chance you can be cheated.

She adds, 'Even if you are cheated, if you live with love you will live like a god on planet earth. On the other hand, even if you are not cheated, if you live without love, your life will be dry and dead.' Only with love, trust, compassion and faith can you have real fulfillment in life.

A man who is emotionally mature with an open heart is the one qualified to receive the healing. I can reach out my hand to you to help you, but you must reach out your hand to grab mine. Open your heart and receive the healing energy of the Divine.

Absorb the energy and be healed by divine grace on every level!

THE PLACEBO EFFECT

In India you can see that every village will have small shrines. And most of the shrines are nothing but a small stone under a tree. Under the tree a small stone will be installed and turmeric and some ash and sandal paste will be applied - that will become God.

And you can see hundreds of people going to that stone and getting healed of their physical diseases, mental illnesses and coming out of their problems. Nothing but a simple stone under the tree, worshipped as God, heals the people. Nothing more is required.

So many people go to the river and pray to the river; they go to the sun and pray to the sun. They go to the temples and pray to the gods. There are a few places where they go to the trees and pray to the trees. Trees are worshipped as Gods. Praying to the trees, praying to the stones, praying to the rivers, people get healed. How is it possible? How can this happen?

PLACEBO EFFECT

> The placebo effect is the measurable, observable, or felt improvement in health or behavior not attributable to a medication or treatment that has been administered.
>
> – The Skeptic's Dictionary

Researchers at the Houston VA Medical Center and at Baylor College of Medicine in the United States conducted surprising research to test the benefits of surgery versus the placebo effect on 180 patients with osteoarthritis of the knee. The patients were divided into three groups. One group had the damaged joint removed, the second group had the area surgically washed to remove the damaged cartilage and the third group had fake surgical intervention. Neither the patients nor the surgical team knew which surgery was to be performed.

When the patient was on the operating table, the surgeon opened an envelope with instructions regarding the surgery to perform. The team made incisions on the knee, bent the knee and made all the usual sounds of surgery for those getting the fake surgery in case they were partially conscious. The post-operative care for all three groups was identical. Throughout the two years of follow-up none of the patients was aware of what type of surgery they had. Each group reported modest improvements in pain and mobility and the placebo group actually reported greater recovery than the other two groups at certain points during the two year monitoring period.

"I was initially very surprised," Dr. Bruce Moseley, an orthopedics professor at Baylor who performed both the real and placebo surgeries in the study, told United Press International. "I associate placebo effect with pills."

Moseley stated that the patients responded so positively because they believed they had been helped by surgery, which seemed to make a difference in their perception. "In my simple surgeon's explanation of this, the magnitude of the placebo effect is directly proportional to the patient's perceived intervention."

"The physician's belief in the treatment and the patient's faith in the physician exert a mutually reinforcing effect; the result is a powerful remedy that is almost guaranteed to produce an improvement and sometimes a cure."

- Petr Skrabanek and James McCormick, Follies and Fallacies in Medicine, p. 13.

We can see that it is not only or necessarily the medicine or intervention that heals a patient but the faith, the *shraddha*, that all involved have for it that brings about healing. It is what the patient believes that makes the difference. The very *shraddha* works miracles in human beings.

Nocebo Effect

A nocebo is something that should be harmless but actually causes ill symptoms or side effects due to the suggestion or patient's belief that something is harmful.

"In one experiment, asthmatic patients breathed in a vapor that researchers told them was a chemical irritant or allergen. Nearly half of the patients experienced breathing problems, with a dozen developing full-blown attacks. They were "treated" with a substance they believed to be a bronchodilating medicine, and recovered immediately. In actuality, both the "irritant" and the "medicine" were a nebulized saltwater solution."

- Hippocrates, November, Vol. 13, No. 10.

WHY DOES THE PLACEBO EFFECT WORK?

The placebo effect works because of the *shraddha*, the faith that the person has on a particular thing to produce a certain result. We may not realize that we have the faith. Consciously or unconsciously, we believe that the 'medicine' will work. We believe in the power of whatever we are doing or taking but we do not understand the science behind it.

The science behind *shraddha* is what forms the basis of Nithya Spiritual Healing. Nithya Spiritual Healing is a proven science of healing and the science of how it works is based on *shraddha*.

SHRADDHA

Shraddha is loosely translated as faith but actually it is not just faith. *Shraddha* is also not just sincerity. *Shraddha* is actually much higher than faith or sincerity.

To have *shraddha* means to have an understanding of the concept, experience full sincerity towards and belief in it, and express the courage to execute the understanding in one's life. It is not just 'very sincerely and blindly following'.

Shraddha is sincerity plus understanding and expressing that understanding with courage even before we fully experience the desired outcome in our lives.

Shraddha requires that we become integrated, with our intelligence, emotions and spirit aligned towards a particular ideal or belief.

Introduction to Nithya Spiritual Healing Initiation

Chapter 3

Introduction to Nithya Spiritual Healing Initiation

First let me tell you why this Healers' Initiation - why I created this healing system.

The first thing, please understand:

This Healers' Initiation is straightaway related to your enlightenment.

Healing others is only a side effect or a by-product.

All I am trying to do is put you consciously into the deepest level of your Being.

For example, the Life Bliss Program Level 1 - Ananda Spurana Program (LBP Level 1 - ASP) gives you a glimpse of bliss. The Life Bliss Program Level 2 - Nithyananda Spurana Program (LBP Level 2 - NSP) gives you a glimpse of energy or consciousness.

Here, I am trying to put you in the same state permanently. When you go inside your being, naturally you radiate energy and that energy automatically heals others.

One more thing:

Healing is conscious, concentrated love.

Just as the love of a mother cat licking her hurt kitten naturally heals the kitten, in Nithya Spiritual Healing your love heals the person receiving the energy.

Introduction to Nithya Spiritual Healing Initiation

I am going to give you a technique to develop deep and concentrated love.

It is not just a superficial technique. Let me tell you, people tell me that they love the whole world. Loving the world is easy but you cannot love your wife! Here I am trying to create a real concentrated love where you will be honest to your being.

REAL COURAGE IS THE COURAGE TO FACE ONESELF

Vivekananda calls his disciples as *dheeraaha*. Here I also address you as 'Courageous ones'. You may ask what courage is needed to take the Healers' Initiation.

Be very clear: To conquer others you don't need courage. A person who kills others does so because he is afraid he will be killed by them. So, before they kill him, he kills them.

What really needs courage is to kill your mind and your false ideas about yourself. In the Healers' Initiation, you are conquering yourself, your mind. That is why I am calling you all *'dheeras'* - the courageous ones.

DAKSHINAMURTHY SWAMIGAL

Let me tell you a true story about inner strength and courage:

In Tamil Nadu, there was a great saint called Dakshinamurthy Swamigal. He never wore clothes; he lived naked.

There was a king at that time, a popular local king by the name Bharani. Bharani means a person who has killed one thousand elephants. The tradition at that time was that if you kill a thousand elephants, the poets will sing the bharani *in your praise and glory. The royal poet sang* bharani *for the king. As it happened, the poet had a chance to meet Dakshinamurthy Swamigal. The poet was deeply impressed by the great master and he sang the same thousand verses of* bharani *on Dakshinamurthy Swamigal.*

Another poet who was jealous of this royal poet told the king there was not just one bharani *which was dedicated to him but that the royal poet had sung the* bharani *for someone else also.*

The king was shocked and asked to whom the bharani *was sung. The poet said that it was for a beggar who was sitting under the nearby banyan tree.*

The king was infuriated and said, 'How dare the royal poet sing the bharani *on someone who lives naked, a beggar who does not even wear clothes!'*

The royal poet was summoned and asked to give an explanation. He said, 'Oh king, please come once to see him and then you can decide as to what I have done is right or wrong.'

The king went with all his paraphernalia: elephants, soldiers, horses and the like. The scene was a dramatic contrast between the two. On one side was a beggar sitting under the banyan tree. On the other side was a king full of ego and pride walking towards that tree.

The king went near Dakshinamurthy Swamigal and saw him at close quarters. Dakshinamurthy Swamigal was sitting silently, continuously radiating bliss. He straightaway gave the king a long, penetrating stare. The king was shaken to his very core because no one in his life had ever looked straight into his eyes like that. Only he had given the straight look to others. No one had had the courage to look back into the king's eyes.

Just then, something happened, and the king became so silent. Dakshinamurthy Swamigal closed his eyes and just indicated by a motion of his head, 'Sit'. Because the king sat, the whole army sat. They were just sitting for hours. Not even a single thought entered the king's mind. A whole day passed. One day, two days, three days passed. The king and his entourage continued to sit in silence – no food, no water, nothing.

Dakshinamurthy Swamigal opened his eyes on the third day and simply said, 'Now you can go.' Suddenly the king got a glimpse of consciousness and wondered what had happened to him. He himself didn't realize how the time had passed but he was in deep bliss and peace.

The king told the poet, 'It is not the bharani *that you can sing for this great sage. Sing the* bharani *for him!' (song of glory when a person kills 10,000 elephants)*

Killing 10,000 elephants is easy, but killing the mind is very difficult.

HEALERS' INITIATION - A MARRIAGE BETWEEN YOU AND THE DIVINE

Here you are entering into your mind, so you are courageous. That is why I say, *'Dheeraaha*, welcome!' See, after LBP Level 1 - ASP, at any time you can break from all this and say good-bye. But taking the Healers' Initiation is a commitment.

We are going to get married! Not just for one life, but for life after life. One thing you should understand that happens during the initiation is that the master takes up the responsibility that even if he leaves his body before the disciple's enlightenment, he will set him up with another master or continuously give him visions and guide the disciple to the Ultimate. It is a *bandha*. It is a commitment that you make with yourself, not to me. It is not just a life-long but a death-long commitment. It is a commitment between you and your *Atman*.

Healing - A Means to Go Beyond Your Ego

The first thing is that it is very important that you use this wonderful intelligence and energy that I am going to give you in a proper fashion. It is like giving a knife in the hands of a child. Of course, it will not harm anybody when used improperly in this case. The energy can never harm anybody because energy *is* intelligence. But when you don't use this wonderful intelligence in a proper and productive fashion, it is a disrespect to it.

Secondly, I want to adequately warn you about how to handle the tremendous respect that will come your way once you start spiritual healing for the public. Our healers are respected so much amongst the public. It is like children enjoying the father's wealth! The healers need to have the maturity to handle the respect that they get from people and from me.

Vivekananda beautifully says, 'It is not a big job to get name and fame, but it is a big job digesting it!' You can do any nonsensical thing and get popular overnight! But to be able to digest the popularity is the tricky part.

Introduction to Nithya Spiritual Healing Initiation

Handling Name and Fame

Let me tell you a story:

In a South Indian temple, the deity's idol was customarily brought out of the temple on the back of a donkey in a big procession around the town for people to see. On one such occasion, as the procession moved, the donkey was excited to see people bowing low before it, performing arathi *(offering of lights) and offering sweetmeats. It did not consider that all the attention was for the blessed deity that it carried. It suddenly thought to itself that it might have become enlightened overnight!*

You see, thinking that you are enlightened is the most dangerous thing ever. Once you become enlightened, you will neither have the doubt whether you are enlightened nor the ego that you are enlightened. This is the actual enlightened state. If you have either the ego that you are enlightened or the fear that you may not be enlightened, be very clear, you are not enlightened.

Anyhow, the donkey thought that it was enlightened and started to swagger and look contemptuously upon the other animals in the streets. It decided that it no more needed to carry the heavy burden on its back. It shook the deity off its back. Then, the real puja *(worship) for it started! It got beaten like anything.*

As long as you are aware that you are an instrument of God, you are perfectly safe. When people touch your feet, remember that they are actually prostrating to the *mala* that is around your neck. If you start thinking that the *mala* is too heavy and there is no need to wear it, the problem starts and you are entering a dangerous zone!

Be very careful as to where you are headed with your ego. You can carry it either towards enlightenment or towards something else. With enlightenment, you will have the power along with maturity to handle the power. With something else, you are only in trouble. Remember: The path to darkness and the path to light are the same, only the directions are different!

There is a story told by Ramakrishna:

Through meditation, a sannyasi *acquired the power to control the god of rain, Varuna and the god of wind, Vayu. Once a thunderstorm raged and many ships were caught in the perilous sea. By his powers, the sannyasi stopped the storm abruptly. Had the storm abated on its own, the ships would have slowly regained their stability. Since he abruptly stopped it, the ships overturned and the people on board died. He had the power,* shakti, *but not the wisdom,* buddhi, *about how best to use the powers. Because of this, he lost his powers and faced the punishment for the tragedy.*

This is what happens when power comes without maturity. This kind of energy is what we call the unconscious energy. On the other hand, when you possess superconscious energy, you are also bestowed with the intelligence to use it. Unconscious energy comes without the user's manual of intelligence!

Responsibility – The Way To Expand!

Making Responsibility Our Very Nature

Chapter 4

Responsibility – The Way To Expand!

Making Responsibility Our Very Nature

(From Paramahamsa's address at Healers' Initiation, March 2005, Bidadi, India ashram)

I want this healing system to be given free to people. Not only in India, but in all other countries, our healing is offered as a spiritual service. There are 2000 healers who have been initiated till now, and today 160 of you are going to be initiated. Totally there will be 2160 healers. There are already 700 healing centers the world over. Today, 100 more will take shape. Totally there will be 800 centers. 800 centers and 2160 healers will be doing healing as a service because this is a divine cause. This is an opportunity to give to others the great gift that we have received ourselves.

Just think - if I had not happened in your life, would you not have missed something? Some aspect you would have missed, because in some way something has been added to your life - either physical health, or mental relaxation or happiness at the spiritual level. Now, someone has been responsible for bringing you to me and therefore something has been added to your life, is it not?

First, I took up the responsibility of reaching out to people. Then, the next circle took it up, then the next circle, and so on. That is how this movement has reached you. Even if you came to know of me through a magazine, there is someone

Responsibility - The Way to Expand

responsible for running that magazine, isn't it? Should you not feel grateful to them? I have seen many people who worship the ones who introduced them to me!

Just like how people took up the responsibility of introducing you to me, you should take up the responsibility for this to reach more people. Normally we feel responsible for any good that happens in the world. For anything bad that happens, we feel someone else is responsible; and mostly that someone is God! The biggest garbage can in our lives is God! For anything bad that happens, we blame Him. Poor man - He can't even talk back!

Sometime back, there was tuberculosis all over Tamil Nadu. They found medicines and cured it. The officials responsible for eradicating it proudly claimed that they were the ones responsible for curing it. But did they take up the responsibility for the fact that it was allowed to spread all over the town? No! They were actually responsible for the spreading of tuberculosis also, is it not? They should have prevented it. Likewise in our lives, we claim responsibility for any good that happens but don't claim responsibility for anything bad that happens. We simply blame God for it. We take up responsibility with discrimination.

Only if we take up responsibility for everything that happens in our lives, we will start expanding.

When you start living with the attitude, 'I am responsible', your whole life will change. If you sit and analyze each and every incident in your life, you will see clearly that only you have been responsible for them. But we normally pass the buck and blame others for what has happened in our lives. Those who do not wish to progress at all in life may do this. Those who wish to blossom should feel responsible directly or indirectly for everything that happens around them.

Vivekananda beautifully says, 'Take as much responsibility on your shoulders. The more responsibility you take, the more you expand. Expansion is the only growth; else you will contract and die.' The more responsibility you take up, the more you grow. Only when you feel responsible for all that is happening around you, you become a leader. Till then you are not even a serviceman, you are a mere hooligan.

State, Not Status

Most of us wait for the status to come in order to take up the responsibility. Be very clear, it doesn't work that way. Only if we take up responsibility, the status will come. Those who wait for the status will not take up responsibility even after they get it. They will simply find another reason or excuse, that's all.

Responsibility is a consciousness. Only those who feel responsibility as a consciousness can become spiritual healers.

Compassion Expresses as Responsibility and Hence Energy

One man asked me, 'How is it that so much energy flows from you?' When you feel compassion towards others' suffering, the whole thing takes the shape of responsibility and expresses itself as energy, that's all. For that matter when anyone takes up responsibility towards the suffering around him or her, they will immediately start radiating energy.

Responsibility - The Way to Expand

There are some already initiated healers here. Tell me, when a person is suffering, if you feel that you are responsible for him, will you ignore him and walk away? No. Even if he refuses, you will give him help, is it not?

Some people say, 'We feel embarrassed when people don't believe what we say about our spiritual healing.' As if people believed me when I first started talking! Whether you believe it or not, I had 'two and a half' people in my first meditation program. I include the 'half' because one man used to sleep most of the time! This was how this whole movement started.

How many disciples did Jesus Christ have? 12. How many disciples did Ramakrishna have? Only 16. Just 16 of them started the movement. Because they took up the responsibility, it expanded; understand that. Of course, you should be careful about the laws of your country with respect to healing and obey them.

Be very clear: You can stand up only if you feel responsible for people's spiritual upliftment. You should be able to say that you will do whatever you can towards it. Understand deeply this concept – when you stand up with responsibility, you expand and the divine energy flows through you. Can air flow through a blocked bamboo? A blocked bamboo will help only to carry a corpse. That same bamboo when cleared of its blocks will become a flute! As long as you are self-centered, you will serve as the blocked bamboo that carries the dead body. When you are free from ego and stand up with responsibility, *atma vikaasa* or expansion happens, and you become like the bamboo flute. Then, like how the air that enters the bamboo leaves it as music, so too will the air that enters you flow as energy!

A Cognitive Shift

When you take up responsibility, a cognitive shift happens in you; your mental setup changes. You are currently living like a slave. You work eight hours in your office. The same eight hours, if you take up responsibility and work, things will become very easy for you.

Take, for example, a doctor who has private practice and a doctor who works for the government. The former will appear to be flowering and happy all the time with no grudge or grumble. But the latter will appear to be under some load all the time. This is because the former stands up with responsibility while the latter does not. If he too stands up with responsibility, the whole scene will change for him. Else, he will keep looking at his watch to see if it has struck 5pm for him to leave. For him, only the first of every month will be sweet since it would be payday! From the second to the thirty first, it will be sour. He sacrifices thirty days of his life for that one day of joy. A sense of personal responsibility can help turn around any situation and achieve great things.

When you collectively stand up with responsibility, you become a solid force. Until then, you remain a burden for yourself and for others. We often think that we are after all in an ordinary post and when our higher authorities at work are not taking up responsibility, why should we take it up!

Let me tell you, in an office, when a sweeper does all his duties perfectly, he will inspire people. You see, the head of the organization has to be responsible anyways. No credit is given to him for that!

Responsibility - The Way to Expand

Ramakrishna beautifully says, 'A *sannyasi* has to think of God. No credit is given to him for it. A *samsari* (householder) is given credit every time he thinks of God! When a *sannyasi* forgets God for even a moment, it is a sin, whereas when a *samsari* thinks of God even for a moment, it is a great thing.' In the same way, a leader has to be responsible. No credit is given to him for being so; whereas if a sweeper is responsible, he can inspire an entire institution.

There is a higher chance of people at a lower post inspiring others through their sense of responsibility than people at a higher post.

Therefore, don't wait to get a post to become responsible. Secondly, don't think that you are in a lesser post, and therefore you need not be responsible.

Thirdly, allow the cognitive shift to happen in you.

Allow a change in the mental setup to happen in you. Currently, our mind is in a state of *mithyam* (ephemeral); that is, all the time it is searching for worries and sorrow in the outer world. If you deeply analyze yourself, you will realize that if you are enjoying intensely, you will suddenly be engulfed with a feeling of fear that there is nothing to worry about. Then you immediately start thinking of things to worry about. You will feel that you have lost something and therefore start recollecting all your worries. *Mithyam* means going in search of sorrow and the ephemeral; going in search of that which is not there. Now, we have to change the state of the mind from *mithyam* to *nithyam* or eternal (in the present moment). This is called the cognitive shift. This will happen when you stand up saying that you are responsible.

For just 24 hours, if you stand up with this feeling, things that were lying unfinished for which you blamed others will get finished, and your entire life will change and blossom with a new sense of happiness. A new kind of ecstasy will engulf you. You will become a natural leader and life will become a celebration!

There is a beautiful story on Buddha. It is said that when Buddha went to beg, he would appear like a king and the kings who gave him alms would appear like beggars! Seeming like a beggar or a king is not because of your status or the property that you own. It is because of the state inside you. When you take up responsibility for the entire cosmos, you will expand and look like a leader. Even when a leader is sitting on his throne, if he points his finger at others for responsibility, he will appear small. The state is that which gets the status; the status can never get the state. The state of Nithyananda is different from the status of Nithyananda.

A Commitment to Serve People

If you are willing to look at healing as a service to people, you may take the initiation. The mentality is important. Some of you may say, 'People might not believe what I say. I feel embarrassed to tell them about this.' If you feel truly responsible for their suffering, you will not say these things. You are not going to ask them for money. Why don't you tell them that you have learnt a healing meditation and that they could give it a try? You are sure that there is not going to be any side effect. Also, you are not going to give them any medicine for it. Then what is wrong in suggesting? If you can't even take up this responsibility, then why this gift of energy to you!

Responsibility - The Way to Expand

Vivekananda's motto for his mission was - *atmano mokshartham jagat hitaya cha*. He describes the goal of his mission as, 'For spiritual liberation as well as bringing good to humanity'. He implies that without taking up responsibility for the good of the world, you cannot talk of spiritual liberation.

We all think that once we die, God will send us a separate flight from *Vaikuntha* (heaven); Rambha and Menaka, the celestial beauties will be the airhostesses waiting at the door of the flight! Once we reach *Vaikuntha*, Paramahamsa Nithyananda will be there since we have attended the NSP, and he will give us a ticket and send us in! It is not so. If you live with a selfish motive, no flight will come!

There are a few already initiated healers here. Tell me, when your healing meditation helps a person heal, you feel responsible to have helped him, is it not? At least you feel that your Master has helped, isn't it? The feeling of 'my Master' is all right. It is not counted as ego. It will not disturb you because the moment you feel that he is 'your Master', He will take care of your ego. As Lord Krishna says, it is alright for the *gopikas* to say 'my Krishna'; it is not counted as ego.

Ok now, when you feel that 'your Master' has helped the person in the healing process, when the same person is suffering also, should you not feel that 'your Master' has not helped him? For you not to feel this, what should you do? Spread this message of spiritual healing, that's all. Let it reach as many people as possible.

Do you know the story of how Pandarinathar came to Pandaripur? Let me narrate: In the place called Pandaripur, there was a boy who did immense service to his parents and others. Lord Krishna took the form of Pandarinathar and came to see him. It was raining and the boy was attending to his parents.

Krishna asked to be allowed inside but the boy asked him to wait until he had finished attending to his parents. Krishna said that it was raining and slushy where he stood. The boy threw a block of brick and asked him to stand on it! Till today, Pandarinathar is worshipped on a brick-block in that place! To see the consciousness of responsibility of the boy, God himself came down. That is why I tell people: When you stand up with responsibility, energy will automatically flood you!

Feeling that you are responsible is the greatest quality. You all tend to think that you came for two days, had a good time, Master energized you on the forehead (on your *Ajna chakra*) and that it is enough. For this mentality, the energy will last for a few days, that's all. Only for those who take up responsibility, the energy will be there forever.

EGO VERSUS RESPONSIBILITY

When you stand up feeling responsible, your problems will dissolve; a new intelligence will awaken in you. Don't think that by thinking this, you are being egoistic. Ego is different from responsibility. When you feel responsible, you will take the initiative; you will not feel egoistic. Only when you think that you would have done better than the other person, ego will come into play and you will then not take up responsibility also.

HEALERS ARE MY HANDS

I say that healers are my hands. When I say 'I', don't think I am talking about this six-feet tall Nithyananda. I am talking about the *prapancha shakti,* the cosmos. When I say that the same energy that is flowing in me will flow through you, it is not an assurance, it is a promise!

RESPONSIBILITY IS NOT SERIOUSNESS - THE WORLD IS BUT A DREAM

Being responsible is not becoming serious. Sincerity is different from seriousness. When you become serious, you are only feeding your ego. When you are sincere, you understand about life and do not attach undue importance to anything at the cost of something else. You are able to approach life with a youthful enthusiasm, spontaneity and innocence.

A child's world is full of, 'He took away my pencil!' 'He hit me!'... 'She is not giving me my chocolate!' We have lived this stage in our life and only then reached here. How does it feel when you think back about this? It appears comical now, doesn't it? It appears to be madness! We feel how much we bothered at that age for these little things.

After this, let's fast forward a bit, to when we were five or six years old. At this age we fight for, say, a geometry box. When we were a few years younger, we fought for a pencil and now we are fighting for the geometry box.

You grow up further. Now, if your best friend moves very closely with somebody else, then you can't bear that! Now if we think back about this we only feel like laughing.

All of you here are adults. If I asked some of you elderly people about the problems of youth, about relationships perhaps, the problem will hardly appear of a serious nature to you. This is because you have passed that age.

Just like this, there is a state that is beyond all these states. It is the state of experiencing bliss. It is an experience that goes beyond all the states of life.

Take another example: Say tonight someone whom you loved passes away. Someone has murdered him. Even when you read this, how much grief and trouble you feel! He has passed away. Through the night you are crying. In the morning when your mother gives you a nudge and says, 'Wake up' and you wake up and realize, 'Oh! This is only a dream' how much peace is born within you! From this, we can understand a small technique for living life also – 'When the dream disappears, peace is born.'

Ramakrishna Paramahamsa says, 'This whole world is merely a dream.' How many people can accept this? You look at this world as reality because you have experienced it so.

We can accept things only when we experience them. The things that we have not experienced, we cannot accept. The only way to accept is to experience. The only solution is to go within you and experience that bliss.

In our youth, the problems of childhood appear comical. In our old age, the problems of youth appear comical. When we realize the Ultimate and look at the world from the *Ananda Gandha* (the point where the Formless merges into the form) experience, everything will appear to be playful. You can play the game of life beautifully, completely neck-deep in it, yet completely unaffected by it.

What is Nithya Spiritual Healing Initiation?

Chapter 5
What is Nithya Spiritual Healing Initiation?

WHAT IS NITHYA SPIRITUAL HEALING INITIATION?

> In Nithya Spiritual Healing Initiation (NSHI), you are initiated by Paramahamsa Nithyananda to become a channel for the same divine cosmic energy that he embodies, to flow through you to the person receiving the healing.

GENESIS OF NITHYA SPIRITUAL HEALING

The genesis of Nithya Spiritual Healing lies in the first self-healing experience as related by Paramahamsa.

FIRST HEALING EXPERIENCE

I left home at the age of 17 and spent several years wandering in search of the Ultimate Truth. During my wandering days, I spent many years in the Himalayan regions and more than nine months in Tapovan. From Gangotri, one has to trek to Gomukh first, and from there climb up the mountain-face to Tapovan. Tapovan has no access paths and traveling to and from Tapovan requires extensive acclimatization. Tapovan is considered one of the 'airstrips' to the mystical *shambaala* - enlightened energy field.

I was returning from Tapovan in an army truck. In those trucks there would not be seats, only wooden planks tightened with

What is Nithya Spiritual Healing Initiation?

bolts and nuts. Suddenly the truck went over a big bump and I flew and fell on the wooden plank. My backbone hit the bolt and cracked. The doctors took an X-ray and said that I should take rest for 30 days. 30 days was too long a time for me to stay in one place just taking rest. I did not bother about the doctor's instructions, did not take any treatment and just put my hand on the injured area. That's all. It got healed!

That was when I realized the power of healing that our body carries in itself.

THE DIVINE REVELATION OF THE NITHYA SPIRITUAL HEALING FORMULA

After enlightenment, I was in a place called Nerur, which houses the *jeeva samadhi* (living energy field) of an enlightened master, Sadashiva Brahmendra.

One of my teachers at the polytechnic college where I studied in came to meet me. She had heard about my healing powers. She asked me, 'Why don't you initiate us into your healing system?'

I replied that I knew how to heal myself but didn't know how to initiate another into healing. But she persisted and wanted to be initiated into healing. At that moment, I was sitting close to the *jeevasamadhi* of Sadashiva Brahmendra. I could feel the master's presence.

I was relating with the energy and conveying my situation where the teacher was not ready to leave me without being initiated. Suddenly I heard a sound. When I turned, I saw Sadashiva Brahmendra standing there right in front of me. He gave me a tuft of *darbha* grass and told me to give it to the teacher and tell her to start healing with it. Just as the thought 'how' entered my inner space, the formula for transferring the healing technology was revealed.

I use this divine knowledge to transfer to others the divine experience I myself had. I initiated my teacher as the first Nithya Spiritual Healer.

(This is the history of the unique, effective and divine method of healing, Nithya Spiritual Healing, which has sprung forth from the enlightened consciousness.)

ANANDA GANDHA CHAKRA

It is into the *Ananda Gandha chakra* that the seven *chakras*, the seven energy bodies, and the five *koshas*, all collapse. It is the state in which enlightened masters live. It is the source of all our energy, and the direct connection to the universal cosmic energy. It does not exist in the physical body, but has a metaphysical significance.

When a person with enlightened consciousness initiates a healer, he opens the door to the *Ananda Gandha chakra*, so there is access to the divine energy directly every single moment. When you are in *Ananda Gandha*, you are enlightened because you are one with cosmic energy.

The Master lives in *Ananda Gandha*. This is the *hiranyagarbha* (primal state of the universe before manifestation), the source of all energy of creation. That is why the healing energy is able to give new life, new energy and heal. A connection to the same energy source is established when we are in *Ananda Gandha*.

What is Nithya Spiritual Healing Initiation?

ENTER THE SPACE WITHIN

ज्ञानप्रकाशकं सर्वं सर्वेणात्मा प्रकाशकः ।
एकमेकस्वभावत्वात् ज्ञानं ज्ञेयं विभाव्यते ॥

Jnaana prakaashakam sarvam sarvenaatmaa prakaashakah |
Ekam eka svabhaavatvaat jnaanam jneyam vibhaavyate ||

Vijnana Bhairava Tantra

Staying in *Ananda Gandha*

All things are revealed by *jnana* (knowledge), and the self of all is the knower. By reason of their nature being the same, one should contemplate on the knowledge and the knower as one and the same.

ANANDA GANDHA IN THE CONTEXT OF THE *CHAKRA* SYSTEM

Let me explain to you where the *Ananda Gandha chakra* lies, with the help of the seven-*chakra* system.

The point where all the seven *chakras* collapse is the *Ananda Gandha chakra*.

The path to the *Ananda Gandha chakra* is between *anahata* and *manipuraka chakras*. The *Ananda Gandha chakra* itself does not lie there; only the path to it is there.

Figure 4: Ananda Gandha and the 7 chakras

During Nithya Spiritual Healing, you are consciously going into *Ananda Gandha*. You are in the *jagrat sushupti* (waking sleep) state. You are in the enlightened state.

We saw previously, how according to both science and spirituality, matter and energy are equivalent. It is just the level of subtleness or the frequency of vibration of the energy that decides the nature of the manifestation.

YOUR BODY IS ENERGY VIBRATING AT A PARTICULAR FREQUENCY

Your entire body is only a form of energy. When energy oscillates at a particular frequency, it appears as matter. Your body oscillates at a particular frequency, say 30 units. From 30 units to 1000 units, it appears as matter, as your body. Above that frequency, if you put it in fire, it will melt; if a strong wind blows, it will disintegrate. Below the lower frequency also, the same thing will happen. When your energy vibrates at a particular frequency, it appears as your body. Now, where this energy band collapses, that point is the *Ananda Gandha chakra*. Like how this whole balloon will shrink to one single point when it bursts, all your seven *chakras* will shrink to one point and that point is the *Ananda Gandha chakra*.

Only an Enlightened Master Can Open The *Ananda Gandha Chakra*

All other *chakras* are gross and can be opened by meditation. For example, if there is a bolt of a certain size, you can use a suitable ordinary spanner and turn it. If the bolt is slightly smaller, you can use a smaller spanner and turn it. If it is very tiny, like in a watch, then you cannot handle it in the usual way. You need a person who is specialized in handling it. He will use the appropriate instrument to handle it.

In the same way, with the seven major *chakras*, you yourself can meditate and open and energize them. But this *Ananda Gandha chakra* is such that only an enlightened master can open it. It is very deep and very subtle. With this healing initiation, we are going to open it.

Ananda Gandha and the Seven Energy Bodies

Let me now explain *Ananda Gandha* in relation to the seven energy bodies. We have seven energy bodies in us, namely physical, *pranic*, mental, etheric, causal, cosmic and *nirvanic*. Right now, you are all in your physical layer, the outermost layer.

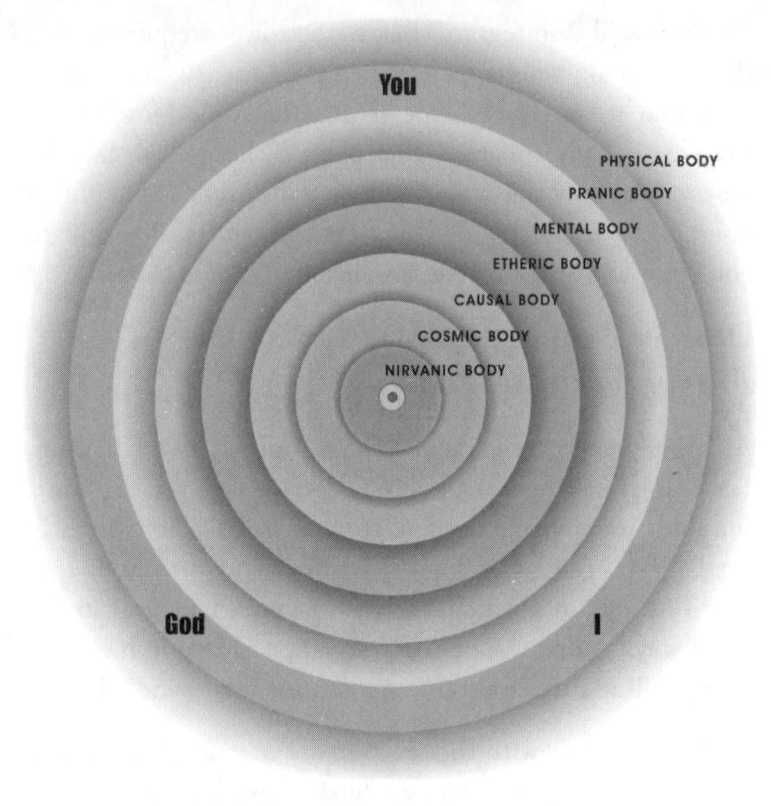

Figure 5: Seven energy bodies and the relation between you, God and I

The distances between you, God and I at the physical layer are considerably large. As we go into the inner layers, you can see that the distance between us decreases and becomes zero at the *nirvanic* or innermost layer. We are all one at the *nirvanic* layer. The *Ananda Gandha chakra* is located in the seventh layer, the *nirvanic* layer. The *nirvanic* layer merges into *Ananda Gandha*. Once this *chakra* is opened, once it is awakened, the energy starts flowing in you continuously.

ANANDA GANDHA AND THE FIVE *KOSHAS*

Now, let me indicate to you the *Ananda Gandha chakra*, with respect to the five *koshas* or sheaths in you.

There are five *koshas* or energy sheaths that are part of our energy system.

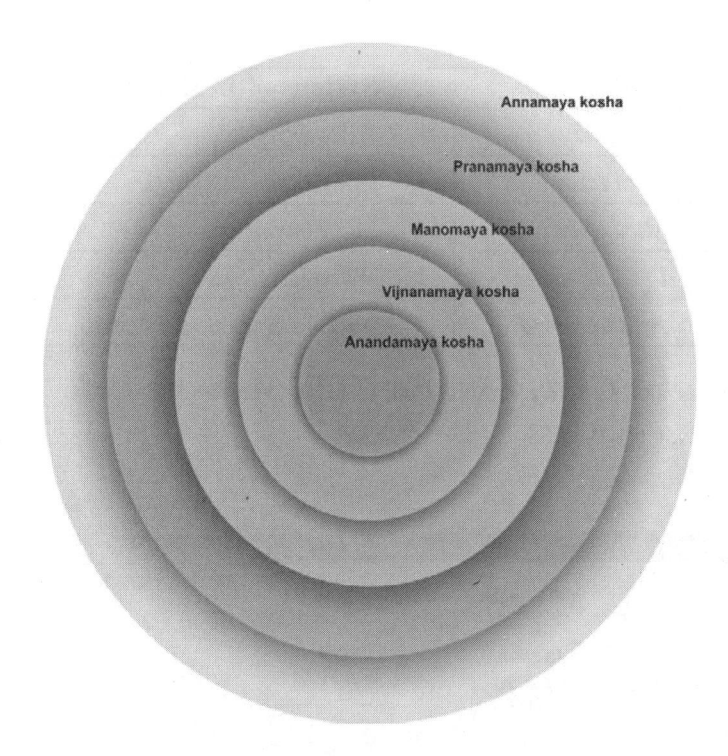

Figure 6: Five koshas *(energy sheaths)*

1. *Annamaya kosha* – gross or physical body
2. *Pranamaya kosha* – energy or breath body
3. *Manomaya kosha* – mental body

4. *Vijnanamaya kosha* – intelligence or visualization body
5. *Anandamaya kosha* – bliss body

Now, where the *anandamaya kosha* or the bliss body touches the *Atman* or Self, there lies the *Ananda Gandha chakra*.

Various systems of healing work on the various *koshas*. The table below shows the relation of the *koshas* to the system of healing.

Kosha	System of healing
Annamaya	Allopathy
Pranamaya	*Pranayama*
Manomaya	Homeopathy
Vijnanamaya	*Ayurveda*
Anandamaya	Nithya Spiritual Healing

ANANDA GANDHA AND THE FOUR STATES OF CONSCIOUSNESS

There are four states of consciousness in us.

When you have 'I' consciousness, along with thoughts, it pertains to the waking state in

	With Thoughts	Without Thoughts
With "I" Consciousness	**Jagrat** Wakeful State — Thinking	**Turiya** Blissful State — State of Full Awareness
Without "I" Consciousness	**Swapna** Dream State — Dreaming	**Sushupti** Unconscious State — Deep Sleep

Figure 7: Four states of consciousness

What is Nithya Spiritual Healing Initiation?

you, the state in which you are right now. In this state, 'I' has more frequency than your thoughts and you can therefore control your thoughts.

When you are without 'I' consciousness but having thoughts, it pertains to the dream state. You will have thoughts in your dreams but you will not be able to control them. In the dream state, your thoughts are at a higher frequency than 'I' consciousness and therefore you will not be able to control the thoughts.

When you are without 'I' *consciousness* and not having any thoughts, you are in the deep sleep state. In this state you have neither 'I' consciousness nor thoughts.

Currently, you are aware of only these three states. However, there is a fourth state, which you have never experienced in your life: when you have 'I' consciousness, but you have no thoughts! This is what is called the 'Zero TPS state'. TPS is Thoughts Per Second. This is what I call the *samadhi* state, *Ananda Gandha, nirvana, Nithyananda* state or Enlightenment. You will have complete awareness but you will not have any thoughts.

THE TIME SHAFT

The shaft (Figure 8) in the center represents 'time'. At any given time, the greater your TPS or Thoughts Per Second, the further you are from consciousness of the present moment and you are simply worrying about the future. By doing this, the present slips into the past, without you ever getting a glimpse of or experiencing the bliss of the present.

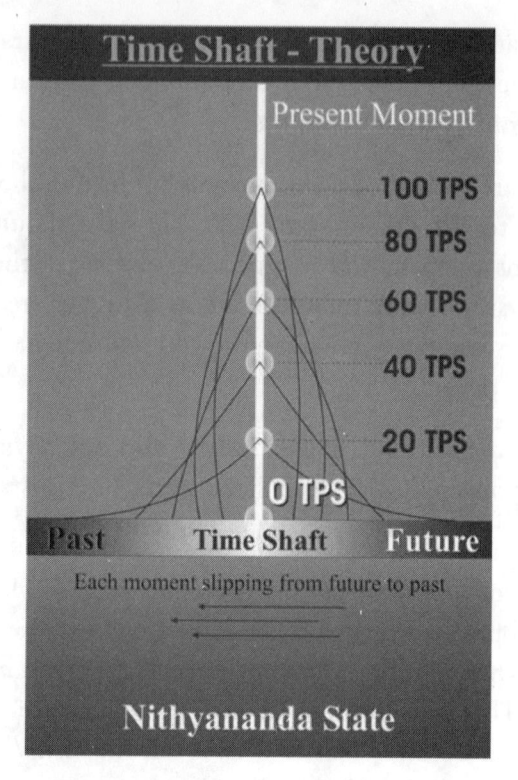

Figure 8: Time Shaft

When your TPS comes down, you enter more and more into the present, getting a clearer vision of the past and the future. Familiar incidents from even past births and intuitions of the future start to surface in you. When this happens, be very clear: for those few moments, your TPS has dropped and you are more in the present.

When your TPS is zero, you can clearly see the entire past and future. Now, by my initiating you into Nithya Spiritual Healing, a short-cut will be created so that your consciousness will simply slip into the present or *Ananda Gandha*.

What is Nithya Spiritual Healing Initiation?

DISCOVERING THE RIGHT KEY

To get this *Ananda Gandha* experience, it took me nine years. When I told this to one of my disciples, he said, '*Swamiji*, you did not have a guru like Nithyananda, that's why it took you that long!' Truly, because I did not have a guru, I played with thousands of techniques and it took me nine years to discover the master technique.

One man asked me, 'When it took you nine years, how is it that you are saying we will attain it immediately?'

Please understand: It took me nine years because I was having 10,000 keys to try and open one lock. Once I found the correct key, it took no time to open it. Now, I have the correct key! All I have to do is give it to you and it will take you one second to open, that's all! You need not waste nine years for it. But if you imagine that it will take you nine years, then even at the end of nine years, nothing will happen!

MASTER CAN SIMPLY PULL YOU INTO *ANANDA GANDHA*

The point where you lose your body consciousness is *Ananda Gandha chakra*.

Ananda Gandha chakra for the whole world actually lies in a single point! The point where the idea of length, breadth and height disappears is *Ananda Gandha chakra*.

The point where the concept of time collapses is *Ananda Gandha chakra*.

The point where the idea of gravity disappears is *Ananda Gandha chakra*.

Imagine that you are an ant on a big iceberg trying to bore its way to the water beneath. No matter how much effort you use or however many births you spend trying, you will only be doing the *tapasya* (penance) of boring the hole without success. But a master, who is in the water (energy) already, can simply drill a hole through the ice from the water beneath and just suck you in. The ant can also enter the water and enjoy! This is exactly what happens during the Healers' Initiation. Instead of you trying to make your way through from the top of the ice, I drill a hole and pull you in!

THE 21- MINUTE CYCLE

When you are very deeply into meditation, you will lose your body consciousness at one point. That point is the *Ananda Gandha chakra*. One 'energy cycle' lasts 21 minutes. If you do the *Ananda Gandha* meditation for 21 minutes, you have to touch the *Ananda Gandha chakra*. When you meditate for 21 minutes, at some point, you will lose your body consciousness, and you will feel only awareness. That is when you have touched the *Ananda Gandha chakra*.

Slowly, when you realize you have lost your body consciousness, you will then try and assert your body and feel it once again. If you feel this once during the day, it is enough.

Nithya Spiritual Healing is a two-in-one technique. You will feel *ananda* and the person receiving the healing will also get healed. That is why this is the ultimate technique.

Some of our other meditation techniques also give this experience but the *Ananda Gandha* meditation gives it consistently and scientifically.

What is Nithya Spiritual Healing Initiation?

You can do certain supportive meditation techniques for *Ananda Gandha* meditation. One such technique is *Shakti Dharana* meditation. It will create a beautiful energy flow in you.

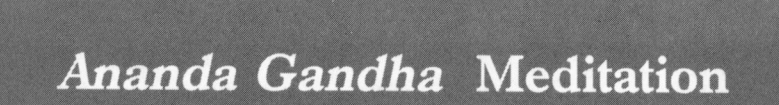

Ananda Gandha Meditation

Chapter 6
Ananda Gandha Meditation

Please close your eyes, sit straight and cross-legged on the floor. Those of you who can't sit on the floor may sit on a chair.

Start visualizing the Master's laughing face in the region between your *anahata* and *manipuraka chakras* which is the path to *Ananda Gandha chakra*. Deeply meditate on that area. You will feel energy flowing from that area. Relax into it. Feel the body flowering. Visualize your whole body smiling, not just your face. Feel your body blossom. Feel the joyous smile from the bottom of your stomach.

Let your thoughts come back to *Ananda Gandha,* if your mind has wandered anywhere. Think of the Master's laughing face again. Drop the face when you start feeling the energy sensation in *Ananda Gandha*. Relax slowly into the flow of energy. Do not try to create, sustain or destroy any thoughts. Just relax into the energy.

You see, if you use any *mantra* to meditate, you will possibly reach the etheric body, the fourth layer of our energy bodies. Only if you meditate and pray on pure energy like in *Ananda Gandha* healing prayer meditation, you will cross the *nirvanic* body, the seventh layer and go inwards.

I tell you to think of me at the start of the meditation, so that you go right into the etheric body because of the visualization. Once you are in the etheric layer, you can drop the visualization of my face and proceed further inwards. My face is like a gateway to the etheric body. Only to get to the etheric body, I ask you to visualize my face.

In the *Ananda Gandha* initiation, the Master is actually pulling us into the state of *samadhi* He is always in.

> *Samadhi* is that in which 'I' consciousness and Supreme consciousness become one. It is without duality and full of bliss, and therein remains only supreme consciousness.
>
> *Upanishad*

> As a crystal of salt thrown into water dissolves in water and becomes one with water, so the state in which unity of 'I' consciousness and supreme consciousness is achieved, is called *samadhi*.
>
> *Upanishad*

There are two types of *samadhi*: *savikalpa samadhi* and *nirvikalpa samadhi*.

Savikalpa samadhi is when you drop attachment to all forms, except the form of the Master or God. For example, Ramakrishna dropped attachment to all forms except to the form of mother Kali.

Nirvikalpa samadhi is when you drop attachment to all forms. For example, Ramana Maharishi did not have attachment to any form.

Savikalpa samadhi is easy to practice but in the end, to realize the ultimate, you have to drop the attachment to that last form and that is tough.

Nirvikalpa samadhi is difficult to practice but realizing the ultimate through this technique is seamless.

Ananda Gandha Meditation

> When the deepest concentration on the supreme *Brahman* also disappears by itself within, there arises *nirvikalpa samadhi* - in which all latent impressions of feelings are eliminated.
>
> Upanishad

The Master is in the state of *nithyananda* – eternal bliss. In that ultimate state, He transcends the limitations of time, space, form and mind. So, from this highest state of consciousness, He can pull us up from the state of *maya*, the fantasy world and emotional imbalances we are caught in.

Ananda Gandha initiation is a beautiful technique designed by the Master, where you first visualize the smiling face of the Master, and fall into *savikalpa samadhi*; his laughing form just pulls you into *Ananda Gandha*. Then, you drop the form as the energy flows through you. You make a quantum leap into *nirvikalpa samadhi* effortlessly.

A lotus blooms just by the penetrating rays of the sun. The *kumudam* (an Indian water lily) flower blooms with just the rays of the moon. Similarly, the *Ananda Gandha* of the devotees blooms with just the presence of the Master!

Now, we will enter into *Ananda Gandha* meditation.
(*The group does the* Ananda Gandha *meditation.*)

After the meditation, a question from the audience: Master, I had a bodyless experience while meditating just now.

Yes, that is the indicator that you really entered into *Ananda Gandha*. If you are able to drop into *Ananda Gandha* with a bodyless experience, it is enough for that whole day. That energy will not allow anything to shake you.

Shakti Dharana Meditation
A Supportive Meditation for Healers

Chapter 7

Shakti Dharana Meditation

A Supportive Meditation for Healers

This technique is taken from *Tantra Shastra* (science of liberation). It is a beautiful technique to relate with the Guru.

It is ideal to practice this meditation at night just before you go to sleep. This can also be done in the morning but it must be followed by at least 15 minutes of rest, as you would otherwise be in a state of stupor or drunkenness. This meditation leads to your merging with the energy of Existence. It is a prayer that can transform you. When you are transformed, the whole of Existence is transformed.

The importance of *Shakti Dharana* meditation is that it takes you to the entrance of the fourth state of *turiya* (Fig. 7), where you are in a state of full awareness but without thoughts.

Nithya Spiritual Healing service should not be done on a day when you have not done *Shakti Dharana* meditation the previous night.

MEDITATION INSTRUCTIONS

Stand on your knees and balance yourself well. Please don't sit on your haunches. You have to maintain a standing *vajrasana* (refer picture on next page) posture. Close your eyes and raise both hands upwards with palms facing skywards. Tilt your head slightly upwards.

In this position, feel Existence flow through you. Visualize that a light-beam of Existence is flowing through you. You can visualize my blissful face to start with. Just as a miser is at the peak of his energy when counting money or a lover is at the peak of his energy when he is with his beloved, so also is a Master at the peak of his energy when laughing or smiling. That is why I tell you to remember my blissful, smiling face and allow the energy to flow through you. Also, it is better that you think of me than allow your mind to wander and think of something else!

As the energy of Existence flows down your arms, you will feel a tingling sensation, a gentle vibration, or a slight tremor in you. It would be as if a tender leaf is dancing in the breeze. Just allow the tremor to happen, help the tremor and let your whole body vibrate with the energy. Just allow and help whatever happens to happen. You might feel the merging of the earth below and heaven above, the merging of the male and female energies. You might feel that you are floating or merging. Drop yourself completely. There is no 'you'. You have simply dissolved.

Allow yourself to merge with Existence. After two or three minutes when you feel that your Being is completely filled with the energy of Existence, bend down, rest on your elbows and forearms and kiss the earth or at least let your face touch the ground. You become a medium or a passage for the divine energy to unite with the energy of the earth. Allow all your

Shakti Dharana Meditation

energy to dissipate into mother earth. You may visualize my feet when in this posture.

Now, regain your original posture and repeat this cycle at least seven times.

This meditation improves energy circulation in the body tremendously. All troubles related to the backbone will simply vanish by doing this meditation as the energy goes straight to the *muladhara* chakra which is at the base of the spine.

If you wish, you may do *Shakti Dharana* meditation more than seven times. If you do it less than seven times, you will feel restless and unable to sleep because the energy would not have penetrated all of the seven chakras.

After completing the meditatioHn, go to sleep in the same meditative mood. Just fall asleep and the energy of Existence will be with you. You will be engulfed by it. The sleep that follows this meditation will be intense and dreamless. When you wake up the next morning you will feel fresher, more energetic and more vital than ever before.

This is a very powerful technique and when done consistently, will transform you completely. A new life, a new meaning, a new Truth will start flowing into you. It is a wonderful technique that keeps the connection between you and me alive all the time. It is a technique that takes you again and again to *Parashakti* or the cosmos. You will experience joy and each day will become a celebration!

Nithya Dhyaan

Relax, Rejuvenate, Radiate…

Chapter 8
Nithya Dhyaan

Relax, Rejuvenate, Radiate…

(Up to the age of 11, Paramahamsa Nithyananda subjected himself to numerous meditation techniques. At the age of 12, he had his first deep spiritual experience. From 12 to 21 years of age, he consciously scanned and analyzed the benefits of several techniques. For three years after his enlightenment, he created and perfected a sound technology to reproduce his experience of enlightenment in others. He launched his worldwide mission in 2003 and has been working continuously with millions of people, offering healing and meditation guidance. The essence of this entire inner world research to date is formulated in the **Nithya Dhyaan** meditation technique.

Nithya Dhyaan is a formula and a technique that works on the entire being to transform it and make it ready for the ultimate experience of enlightenment. Each segment of this unique technique complements the other steps to help raise the individual consciousness. It is an everyday meditation for eternal bliss - *Nithya Ananda*.

*All initiated Nithya Spiritual Healers should do Nithya Dhyaan meditation everyday.)

NITHYA DHYAAN MEDITATION EXPLAINED

This is a five-step technique, each step being 7 minutes.

1. CHAOTIC BREATHING
Duration: 7 minutes

Sit in *vajrasana* (sitting on the lower legs with the backside resting on the heels of your feet). Normally in our body, the energy flows from the *sahasrara chakra* (crown center) to the *muladhara chakra* (root center). *Vajrasana* posture helps reverse this and support the upward movement of energy.

Figure 9: Chaotic Breathing

Sit with eyes closed, hands on your hips and breathe chaotically. Inhale and exhale deeply and chaotically, without a particular rhythm. Just focus on the breathing. Your entire being should become the breathing.

An important thing you need to understand is that your quality of breathing changes depending on your state of mind. Your emotions have an impact on the breathing process. When you are in anxiety, your breathing changes. When you are angry, your breathing changes. When you are in tension, the normal advice given is to take a deep breath. And the moment you take a deep breath, suddenly you feel light, more relaxed and the tension is released!

As the breath and mind are inter-related, changing one automatically changes the other. If we were to control our

Nithya Dhyaan

breathing or bring about some change in our breathing pattern, it will directly have an impact on our emotions and our state of mind.

We tend to breathe in a fixed pattern. Our past *samskaras*, past memories locked in our unconscious zone, create a particular type of breathing pattern in our system. As a result, we attract similar emotions and *samskaras*. We get into a vicious cycle where our past *samskaras* create our breathing pattern and the breathing pattern in turn, attracts similar *samskaras* and incidents in the future. This vicious cycle has to be broken.

Nithya Dhyaan begins with chaotic breathing. Since the breathing is chaotic, it has no fixed pattern or rhythm. The mind is not in control since you are breaking the very pattern that forms its existence and expression. Thoughts cannot follow the pattern they have been following so long for so many years.

You have to breathe as deeply as possible and as chaotically as possible. Your entire being should become the breathing. Understand that the breathing has to be deep. The chaotic breathing should not be shallow. Our muscles store all of our past memories in the form of energy bio-memories. The deep chaotic breathing will start releasing the tension in the muscles and engraved memory patterns in your muscles and body parts. Normally our muscles are always under stress. Chaotic breathing will loosen the muscles and start clearing the *samskaras*.

Each emotion within us gives rise to a particular breathing pattern. You might have seen that children breathe deeply and blissfully. But as they grow, they are conditioned by society, picking up from society the perceptions of pain, pleasure, guilt, beliefs, etc. Then the quality of the breathing changes totally. In order to shake this pattern, which has been created due to the habitually suppressed emotions, we have to insert chaos. We have to create turmoil. Inserting another pattern is not the solution.

You have to create utter chaos in your system to dig out all the past impressions. So I don't recommend any rhythmic breathing pattern like *pranayama* in this meditation. Only breathe chaotically. This chaotic breathing will destroy all your past *samskaras*. It is like shaking a tree that is full of dead leaves. All the dead leaves will fall down. Similarly chaotic breathing is like shaking your suppressed system. All the past engraved memories will be released.

Deep chaotic breathing also infuses tremendous oxygen and releases carbon dioxide from the body. It creates hyperventilation and as a result you feel more vibrant and fresh. Through increased intake of oxygen in the blood, automatically more bio-energy is generated in the cells and all aspects of the body come alive. The bio-energy that is generated will start clearing the *samskaras*, leaving you feeling light, energetic and blissful.

2. Intense Humming

Duration: 7 minutes

Figure 10: **Chin Mudra**

Nithya Dhyaan

Continue to sit in *vajrasana*, form *chin mudra* with your fingers, and place your hands on your knees, palms facing upwards.

In this posture, with your mouth closed and lips together, produce a humming sound as intensely as possible, as loudly as possible and as lengthily as possible.

Produce the sound 'Mmmm…' from within your body. If you were to put your face inside an empty aluminum vessel and make a humming sound, the sound generated will be similar to this. Note that this is not 'Humm…' or 'Omm…', it is simply keeping your lips together and producing 'mmm…' sound. The humming should be as lengthy as possible between breaths; it should be as deep as possible (from the navel center) and as loud as possible. There is no need to make an effort to take in deep breaths. The body itself will take breaths when needed.

Put your complete awareness on the humming. Become the humming. Continuously there is talking going on within your mind. Humming is an excellent technique to reduce this inner chatter. Humming lets you feel your body as energy. The moment you start humming, you start feeling light, as if you are floating. You don't feel the heaviness in the body, because humming matches the vibrations of the mind with the vibrations of the body. You start experiencing yourself as energy.

Don't become tense. Just do it in a relaxed manner. Immerse your whole being and energy into creating this vibration. Try to minimize the gap between the humming sounds. After some time, you will feel that the humming continues without your effort and that you have simply become a listener. The body and the mind start resonating with the humming vibrations.

3. CHAKRA AWARENESS

Duration: 7 minutes

Continue to sit in *vajrasana* or sit cross-legged if you wish. Keep your fingers in *chin mudra*. Now take your awareness to each *chakra* (energy center) starting from the *muladhara chakra* (root center) to the *sahasrara chakra* (crown center). These seven energy centers are associated with particular emotions in our being.

Figure 11: Chakra Awareness

These emotions are a result of the engraved memories or *samskaras* which we have accumulated in the past. These *samskaras* block the particular energy center, causing physical and mental disturbances. So in this step we put our complete awareness on each energy center, starting from the base of the spine and moving to the crown. You should become that energy center when you are asked to put your awareness on each energy center. Feel the energy center completely as if your whole being has become that energy center. At the end of this step you will feel energized and light.

4. BE UNCLUTCHED

Duration: 7 minutes

Let me explain the science and concept of being unclutched.

Mind is nothing but a collection of thoughts, one thought after the other, coming in succession. By our very nature, our thoughts are unconnected. They are like bubbles in a fish tank.

Nithya Dhyaan

The bubbles in the fish tank are not connected. They are distinctly separate, but they appear to be connected. In a similar manner our thoughts are not connected though they appear to be connected.

At one moment, you may be thinking about having a cup of coffee and the next moment you may think about some pending office work. There is no real connection between having a cup of coffee and the office work. Both are independent events.

Even if there are two consecutive thoughts about the same event, the thoughts are unconnected as there is no continuity. There is always a gap between thoughts. There is a time of silence between thoughts. The thoughts by their very nature are un-clutched.

The problem happens when we connect these thoughts. We connect these unconnected thoughts and suffer.

The pain which you experienced ten years ago, the pain which you experienced seven years ago, the pain which you experienced three years ago, and the pain which you experienced yesterday are independent events; there is no connection between these events. But you create this imaginary shaft and start thinking, 'My life is a pain.' Your life is neither pleasure nor pain, because the very process of connecting these events is a mistake.

The idea that thoughts are connected is a misconception. And we don't connect all the thoughts. From the millions of thoughts we have, we connect only a few thoughts that we remember and create shafts of pleasure or pain. Those thoughts that we 'connect' are based upon our engraved memories and not on all that our senses actually perceive in any given situation.

Creation of the shaft is the original sin.

If you have created a shaft of pleasure, then you try to extend the shaft because you want to experience the same pleasure again. If you have created a shaft of pain then you try to break the shaft because you want to avoid the pain. You can neither extend the shaft nor break the shaft, because the shaft does not exist!

So the suffering that is created due to the shaft is also unreal. Once you realize this, you are liberated.

Ego is just a name we give to this process of creating a shaft. A sense of continuity is created because of this shaft. This gives us the illusion of the ego. So by our very nature, we are un-clutched. We are enlightened; we just need to realize it.

Once you start accepting life as it flows from moment to moment, bliss happens to you naturally. External circumstances can impact you only if you allow them to. You may think that if we live life in the moment but others around don't, then they will exploit us. Be very clear, nobody can exploit you or disturb you without your silent permission. Once you understand that you are un-clutched, bliss naturally follows and no one can exploit you. When you flow with awareness from moment to moment, you have continuous access to the intelligence, creativity and spontaneity of Existence.

Nithya Dhyaan

यत्र यत्र मनो याति तत्ततेनैव तत्क्षणम्।
परित्यज्यानवस्थित्या निस्तरङ्गस्ततो भवेत् ॥

yatra yatra mano yaati tatta tenaiva tatkshanam |
parityajyaanavasthityaa nistarangas tato bhavet ||

- Vijnana Bhairava Tantra (ancient text of Vedit tradition), verse 129

> Wherever the mind dwells, casting that aside that very moment, the mind becomes supportless, and free from disturbance.

We have two types of identities. One is the identity that we show to the outer world, and the other is the identity that we experience in the inner world, what we think of ourselves. The identity that we show to the outer world is called *ahankar*. The identity which we show to the inner world is called *mamakar*. Both these identities are in constant conflict with each other. The identity which we project to the outer world is always more than what we actually are. The identity which we project to ourselves is always less than what we actually are.

Both these identities are false identities. They are a result of the shaft that we create. They don't exist in reality. As long as we are associating with these identities, we are caught up in *samsara* (worldly activities). Once we go beyond these two identities, we become enlightened.

All the time we are creating, sustaining and destroying thoughts. The process of creation (Brahma), sustenance (Vishnu) and destruction (Shiva) is constantly going on. When we stop creating, sustaining and destroying, we go beyond all three and reach the state of Parabrahman (Supreme Self).

In this step, carry this understanding with you that your thoughts are unconnected, irrational and unclutched. Even if you have thoughts, neither try to suppress them nor try to react to them. Just watch them with the understanding that they are unclutched. Automatically, the witnessing consciousness will start happening in you; you will go beyond the two identities.

Understand that whether you realize it or not, accept it or not, you are already enlightened. By your very nature you are un-clutched. Sit silently and experience the un-clutched state, the state of pure being and bliss. This is the ultimate technique to experience the state of enlightenment.

5. GURU PUJA

Duration: 7 minutes

Figure 12: Guru Puja

Nithya Dhyaan

Just sit silently in a blissful mood and listen to the *Guru Puja mantras* being chanted. Feel connected to Existence and feel the vibrations of the powerful *mantras* within your being. The mantras are a way to express gratitude to Existence and to the Master, for bestowing upon us this great wisdom, which liberates us from ignorance, and helps us attain the state of eternal bliss, *Nithyananda*.

The chanting is in Sanskrit, an ancient, scientific language that has both communication and good vibrations. All other languages have only communication importance. All sounds of all languages can be reduced to the 52 sounds of Sanskrit. By centering ourselves on the vibrations created when chanting these Sanskrit sounds, we can go beyond the words of the mind to the peace of our very being. Even if we don't understand the meaning of the sounds, the phonetic value of Sanskrit will transform our mood and purify our whole body and mind, creating positive vibrations inside our being.

If you are interested in rituals, you can also perform the *Guru puja* (offering gratitude to the Master) in this step by reciting the *mantras* and performing the rituals (For details please refer to the 'Do Guru Puja Yourself' book).

If you are not interested in rituals, you can remain silent and listen to the *mantras*. Even by just listening to the *mantras*, it will do you immense good. *Mantras* carry vibrations which can transform your being and make it blissful.

Practice this meditation technique once a day and you will start experiencing a new dimension of your being. This technique will prepare your body and mind to experience the state of pure consciousness and bliss.

BENEFITS OF NITHYA DHYAAN *

The half hour of Nithya Dhyaan meditation can give you:

- Relief from stress
- Improved relationships
- Inner peace and fulfillment
- Awakened intuition
- Regulated blood pressure
- Enhanced sleep patterns
- Increased clarity
- Increased energy levels for the whole day
- Connection to the divine energy

* You can get your family and friends initiated into Nithya Dhyaan. This will directly contribute to the collective positivity of planet earth, as more and more people will live in an 'un-clutched', liberated way as *jeevanmuktas* (liberated beings). This shift in the individual consciousness will result in a positive shift in the collective consciousness which will in turn impact all of life on earth.

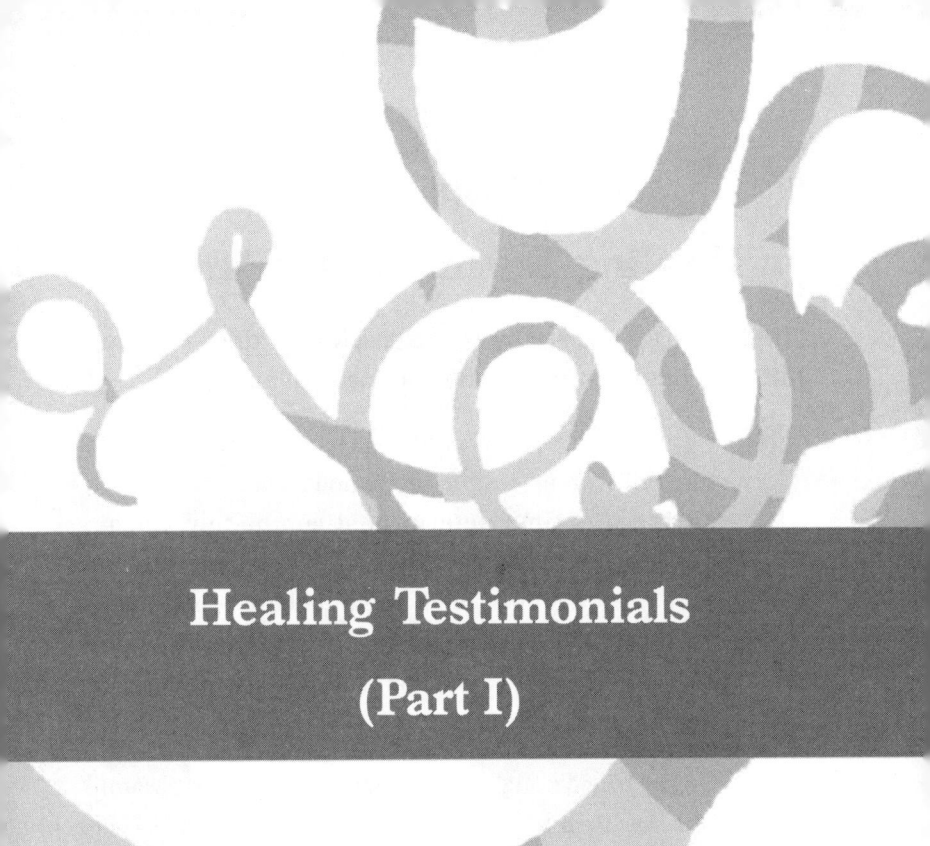

Healing Testimonials
(Part I)

Chapter 9
Healing Testimonials (Part I)

(The healing testimonials by various people refer to Paramahamsa Nithyananda as 'Swamiji' as He is lovingly called.)

1. I was struck with Hepatitis B (jaundice) in 1995, and suffered with no respite for six long years. My appetite during this time deteriorated completely and my digestion completely collapsed. My family tried every available system of medicine but there was no cure. Even the doctors gave up hope. I was living then only on a diet of *rava kanji* (flour soup). I knew that death was around the corner.

   On my friend's suggestion, I agreed to see this 'Swamiji' who was then healing at his Erode ashram. On the very first meeting, I felt a bond being established and I knew without doubt that I would be healed. Swamiji lovingly touched my heart, and voiced that I would be fine. He then asked me to put a pinch of the sacred ash into everything I ate and drank for the next three days.

   I followed this instruction and on the third day itself, my stomach began to feel fine after six long years. Immediately, Swamiji instructed me to eat rice, green chilies and a full South Indian meal and I complied with it. Tears of joy rolled down my face coupled with a feeling of complete blessedness.

   Out of complete gratitude and surrender, I asked Swami Sri Paramahamsa Nithyananda if I could serve as his secretary at the ashram, which Swamiji accepted. Even today I am in good health and bliss and ever ready to serve my divine master. Jai Guru!

-T. N. Dhanasekhar, 45 years, *Vanaprastha Sannyasi* and *ashramite* since 01.01.03

2. I am an agent for healthcare products. In November 2002, I felt giddy and was admitted to Salem Gokulam Hospital. It came as a terrible shock when I was diagnosed with brain hemorrhage. My wife contacted Sri Nithyananda Swami. He promised my wife, 'Just keep your confidence up. I'll take care of him.'

The same day, I was shifted to Sri Ramachandra multi-specialty hospital. Even then the doctors said that since I was in the fifth stage of coma, there was very little hope of recovery. Swamiji came immediately to the hospital and gave me courage and healing. In 12 hours, I amazed the doctors with an unexpected improvement. Later the doctors performed open surgery and corrected the hemorrhage. These operations are successful, only rarely, but in my case the operation was successful.

Swamiji flew from Bangalore to Chennai everyday just to give me healing. This went on for ten days. Now I am perfectly fine. My recovery can be termed a medical miracle. I salute Swami Nithyananda for giving me this new birth!

-Mr. K. Anbalagan, 39 years, Tamil Nadu

3. I suffered from allergic rhinitis and sinusitis for 12 years. It is a well-known fact that there is no permanent cure

for this condition especially in the city of Bangalore where the weather condition is not suitable for such ailments. Swamiji allowed his healing energies to flow over my throat chakra and slowly the stuffiness in my nasal passages and breathing began to improve. I give my thanks to have been fortunate enough to receive healing from a living enlightened Guru.

-Dr. Sangeetha Roy

4. I stay in Salem. I am 67 years old. I had already undergone 3 surgeries and was still suffering from hernia. My doctor told me that a fourth surgery cannot be done because of psoriasis, which doesn't allow the skin to heal properly.

Swamiji gave me courage. In September 2002, in Manipal Hospital, I was admitted for surgery. After the surgery, I experienced a lot of pain. Immediately, Swamiji gave me healing and I came back to normal. By the time I returned home there was no pain or fatigue. The surgeon himself was amazed and said to me, 'Swamiji has saved you' and saluted Swamiji. I will never forget in all my lifetimes the love and compassion of Swamiji who treated me as his own mother.

-Mrs. Punidavathi Thangavel, Tamil Nadu

5. I am a woman of 50 years and was suffering from asthma for the past 10-12 years. I was unable to eat well, lift heavy things or take a long walk. I always complained of indigestion, severe cough with blood, severe backache and a lot of tiredness, which made me a very weak person. I tried all the best possible treatments

like *ayurveda*, homeopathy, allopathy, Kotaikal etc., but could relieve myself of this problem only for a short period. Only a miracle could cure me permanently of these ailments and that miracle did happen to me in the form of Swamiji who cured me through healing and meditation. I met him for the first time on the occasion of *pada pooja* (worship of the holy feet of the Master). I started taking the treatment of healing and meditated regularly for about 15 days.

I am now a fit person who is able to do all sorts of work, be it lifting heavy things or taking a long morning walk, which I was unable to do before. This healing and meditation has made my health good and my mind strong. I can proudly say that I am now one among the healers who can help people come out of their ailments. I am very thankful to our Swamiji whom I regard as God.

-Mrs. Meenal Ramanathan, 50 years

6. I am very grateful to Swamiji for curing me of the ailment of right hand and right thigh pain. I suffered this pain for nearly one and half months and am now cured fully after taking the healing for 21 days.

-P.S. Masilamani

Ananda Darshan

Chapter 10
Ananda Darshan
(Special Feature)

The Master is one with the universal consciousness. He is the formless in form. He is Existence itself. Out of deep love and compassion, through *Ananda Darshan*, he opens Himself completely to all, to experience the universal consciousness through him.

The Master's compassion and divine love is felt by one and all with tremendous intensity. The Master radiates the existential energy around him at all times. At the time of *darshan*, he simply makes himself available with all vulnerability, to instill the divine energy into each person; to plant in each one the seed that can flower and radiate His own fragrance, the fragrance of Existence.

If only we are receptive to the energy, it can penetrate and transform us at the being level. If we can be silent within, free from the grips of our mundane logic, free from thoughts and words, we can simply be a drop in the ocean of bliss that is created here.

The only thing that is expected in return for the unconditional love of the Master is a trusting and receptive approach from our side. If we can just drop our mind for these few hours and fall in tune with the mood that is created, we will be paying our deepest reverence to all of Existence.

There is *kirtan* (music) and dance during *darshan* time. The ecstatic presence of the Master and the energy released during this time transforms the ambience into one of sublime divinity. It is a pure celebration of Existence that can be seen on the faces of and felt by everyone present for this rare and blessed opportunity.

The joy that is created during *darshan* shatters the mind and takes one beyond to feel the oneness with the Whole. The mind is on vacation, freeing the being of its burden, allowing the being to experience what it has always longed to experience; allowing it to experience what it truly is; allowing it to revel in the joy of Existence, of which it is an integral part. The mind vanishes, leaving a void that is filled with an overflowing love for all life.

Darshan is the time when all barriers break – social, economic, and whatever else. It is the time when all identity of self and of the other disappears; everything and everyone celebrates with sheer bliss. Every being shines forth in brilliance, radiating the divinity within.

One can hear all the words spoken by the Master at any other time. But at *darshan* time, he does not speak; he simply shows himself to us. It is the greatest and direct gift from the Master to each one present and available for the experience. If we can be silent and aware, we can see it. If we are caught in thinking and verbalizing, we miss it.

Whether we accept the scene of *darshan* or reject it, we are missing it. If we can do neither and just *be*, without agreeing or disagreeing, without passing any judgment, without trying to verbalize, without any positive or negative feeling, we have caught the thread! If we can just be with the love of realization and not the love of any learning, we can experience it. With no exchange of words, we will find that something in us starts to respond. To millions of people, the *darshan* is a transforming experience.

People around the world who have enjoyed the blessings of *Ananda Darshan* carry wonderful reminiscences. People have had many visions, many instances of healing, many intense spiritual experiences and many ailments pulled out of them at the time of *darshan*.

The energy is perceived by different people in different ways. There is no need to hanker for any experience during *darshan* time. We need to just allow whatever is happening to happen. Then we will be creating a space in us to receive the *darshan*. Energy is intelligence and it knows what to do. There is no need to have any expectation. There is no need to expect experience of any light or emptiness or feeling the energy or anything.

Just being in a prayerful mood at this time is enough; it can transform us more than words can say. Prayerful does not mean asking for things; prayerful means just feeling a deep gratitude towards everything. Of course, the Master always says that we can ask what we feel like after getting the *darshan*, before we get up to leave. He says we could ask any question that we have in our mind, any problem for which we are seeking a solution.

But the moment is so overwhelming and beyond the realms of mundane matter that it becomes difficult to ask anything at all. The moment we are in an asking mood, we miss the whole thing. For us to ask anything, our mind has to step in. And when our mind steps in, we have missed the whole thing.

There have been numerous instances of people saying that when they go near the Master for *darshan*, He simply places His hand exactly in the area of pain or problem in their body. They are shocked. He places His hand exactly in the area that needs to be addressed, even without them telling Him anything. The Master comes out with His love for us and addresses our untold problems.

When questions are asked at *darshan* time, the Master answers with absolute compassion and concern. His answers are different to each person even if the question is the same. It is then that one understands that each being is different, each one's path is one's own, each of us is connected to the Master uniquely, directly and independently. The Master looks into the being of the person and answers the questioner, not the question! For those with complete trust, He simply says, 'I will take care...' These words are not a consolation or for making the person feel good; it is a promise by the Master. It is the assurance of Existence. People shed their anxieties and depression relaxing into this assurance from the Master.

For those few moments, if we can forget our prayers and place our trust in Existence, we can experience more healing and expansion than we could ever imagine possible. Just a little faith that Existence knows what is best for us is enough. If we approach Him with this attitude, we will be able to receive what the Master is trying to give us. It is a tremendous moment for everyone.

Darshan time is a wonderful opportunity to move from communication to communion with the Master. In all the lectures, we keep asking questions for more and more intellectual clarity.

Ananda Darshan

We try to relate with our mind. We collect words and more words at the end of every session. And we come back with more words and questions! We just postpone being with ourselves. *Darshan* time is the time to relate with the Being.

We can allow some experience to happen in us. It is good to try to leave as a different person; a little more evolved.

Every *darshan* is different. The whole beauty of Existence is that it never repeats itself. That is why it is said that God is an artist, not an engineer. Every *darshan* unfolds in a different way, with a new dimension, a new intensity to it, with a new unknown fervor. Every *darshan* seems like the best until the next one unfolds!

The Master's energy transfer to us at the time of *Ananda Darshan* can put us directly into the desireless state. If we are loving and open, it can transform us in more ways than one. A desireless state can also be achieved through consistent intellectual understanding and meditation. But *darshan* time is when one can be directly put into the desireless state purely by the Master's grace.

If we can become completely filled with joy and gratitude, and be present totally, the energy can penetrate us and not only fulfill our desires but take us to a desireless state beyond that. Being in complete joy is actually being in a madly desirous state of nothing in particular! Just intense desire for nothing specific. In this state, we become receptive and open to the Master. We don't have to make any effort for this. We simply have to drop all our effort, that's all! The energy will then take care. It will do the rest. The Existential energy can flow through us and do what is needed if we will just allow it.

Darshan means getting a clear vision, getting a flash of clarity, seeing without a blur. The energy that will be radiated can do miracles at the being level. If we can bring in enough awareness at the time of *darshan*, we will see that amidst the fervor created, amidst the music and dance, there is a pool of serenity that shines forth in the whole scene, a glimpse of the profundity of the oceanic Existence. In the noise that is created, we will find the central chord of vibrant silence that runs through the whole show. Then we will understand the concept of remaining centered and being all-inclusive; of not excluding or renouncing, but encompassing everything, yet remaining centered and being a blissful watcher of the whole show!

After every *darshan*, after every touch, one's intelligence increases, desires acquire more clarity and either get fulfilled or simply drop.

Before the Master, we are completely bare. He sees us at the being level, always. Any attempt to ask anything is actually of no use because we will only be expressing our deep confusion, our deep ignorance. We don't know what it is that we need exactly. He knows what needs to be done to us to take us further.

If we can just allow the music to enter us and express itself in joyful ways, if we can be total and ecstatic, if we can just resonate with the energy, forgetting ourselves completely, we will be emptied of all of our accumulated words and thoughts. Then there will be only emptiness and joy in us when we go near.

In that mood, we are automatically silent inside; we are receptive and loving. We are just bubbling with the inner silence. Then the energy can enter us like a ray, like a flash. It can go deeply into

Ananda Darshan

us and touch us at the seed level and transform us in ways that we don't even know.

Just to be present and watch the Master at the time of *darshan* is an ecstatic meditation by itself. It is a rare opportunity in one's lifetime. It is not worth getting caught in any other detail at this time. Just to be present, aware, without greed but total love and gratitude, is enough.

The Master is so beautiful to look at, so graceful, mesmerizing, as always, and more so during *darshan* time. He shines forth as an ocean of compassion, so fluid and receptive to the helpless pleas and silent calls of the thousands gathered. Each one receives a brush of the Existential energy that stirs the soul, making it soar to merge with Existence itself. One has the potential to lose one's identity and merge with the One.

The Existential energy simply expresses itself and flows through every inch of the Master's form. Just watching Him at this time can bring to us faint glimpses of the divinity it beholds. The more we allow ourselves to dissolve in the whole thing, the more we will resonate with it and the more we can be awakened to the touch and flow of cosmic energy.

This is the time to break our pseudo-identities and social conditionings and celebrate. This is not the time to fasten our seat belts and sit back. The energy will touch us, but we will not be as open to receiving it!

Just being near the Master at this time can cause dissolution into Him. Like a river merging into the ocean, we merge into the Master, who is the oceanic Existence, the formless in form, the universal consciousness. That is why one feels so relaxed and rejuvenated at the end of *darshan*. Sometimes it goes on for long hours through the night. Yet, at the end of it, one feels so vibrant. A shift in consciousness simply lifts one to a higher plane.

When one is near the Master at *darshan* time, unconscious fears, guilt, desires, intense silence, joyful tears, and more surface. One might not even know the reasons for this because these are from our deep unconscious layers which surface by the mere presence and intensity of this cosmic energy.

One does not need to hold back any of the emotions that surface or suppress them. Let them surface freely in the presence of the Master. They will come out in totality. All that we cannot express in words, the deeply engraved unconscious memories that we are not even aware of but that trouble us, will come out as emotions. This is a rare opportunity to be free from these deeply engraved memories. These emotions can be simply wiped out at the root level. The Master's overflowing compassion will wipe them out. The repressive structure that we have built over the years can break at this time, if only we give it a chance.

Whatever happens during *darshan* time happens in totality. We clap our hands, or dance, or laugh or cry – not with any logic, just out of totality of feelings swelling from within. Tears or laughter do not arise from specific reasons of joy or sorrow; they are just expressions of an overwhelming and deep feeling within.

The Being is never given a chance to express itself because of the mind. It has always been repressed and overpowered by the mind. This is a time when the being expresses itself; and when it does, the expressions cannot be framed within the confines of logic. It is pure consciousness expressing, that's all.

Ananda Darshan

Generally speaking, we are not integrated as we think we are. We are really fragments fighting with various aspects within ourselves. While one moment we want one thing, the next moment we want something else. While one moment a particular emotion arises in us, the next moment the opposite emotion surfaces. We are quite chaotic within ourselves although we may appear calm from outside. *Darshan* time is the time to drop this inner struggle and allow the Master to take over and integrate us. He knows us and He will do what is needed if only we relax and let go. *Darshan* time is the time to put aside all our learning, all collected judgments and all conclusions about ourselves and open ourselves to the transforming love of the Master.

With every *darshan*, the Master lights our Being. The real transfer from Him happens at this time. It is the ultimate that He gives to us. He gives us His own Light. Once He lights us, if we allow, we can carry it as our torch wherever we are, wherever we go, in whatever we do. Just one touch is enough; it is an opportunity to know without knowledge, to experience without explanation.

And if the energy has touched us deeply, our life can be transformed forever. A space will be created in us where awareness can enter and dissolve all our questions. There are many doors to the Divine. Once you enter, the experience is the same. The *darshan* opens out all the doors that are there. It is an invitation to the ultimate experience. Each one's door is different, but which door doesn't matter, as long as you have found one.

The energy released during *darshan* time is so intense that it can kindle our intelligence to take us from intellect to intuition. We are mostly caught up in deep unconscious mental patterns of our minds, which pull us repeatedly towards familiar habits of thought and action that result from unconscious reacting. With the power of intuition, we have the ability to tap into the energy of our being and harness it in intelligent, creative decision-making in any sphere of life. The energy at *darshan* time is such that it can open up this intuitive power in us.

We may not understand the depth of what happens during *Ananda Darshan* or the tremendous gift that is given to us, but we can try to be open and enjoy it and accept it with openness; the rest will happen automatically.

Ananda darshan is one time when we can come close to the Master, when we can feel His love through physical nearness, feel the direct transfer of energy from Him. The *darshan* can destroy all that we are not, all that is causing illusion in us, all our borrowed desires that are causing us misery. *Darshan* time is a tremendous opportunity to become one with the universal consciousness, to dissolve into the ocean of bliss!

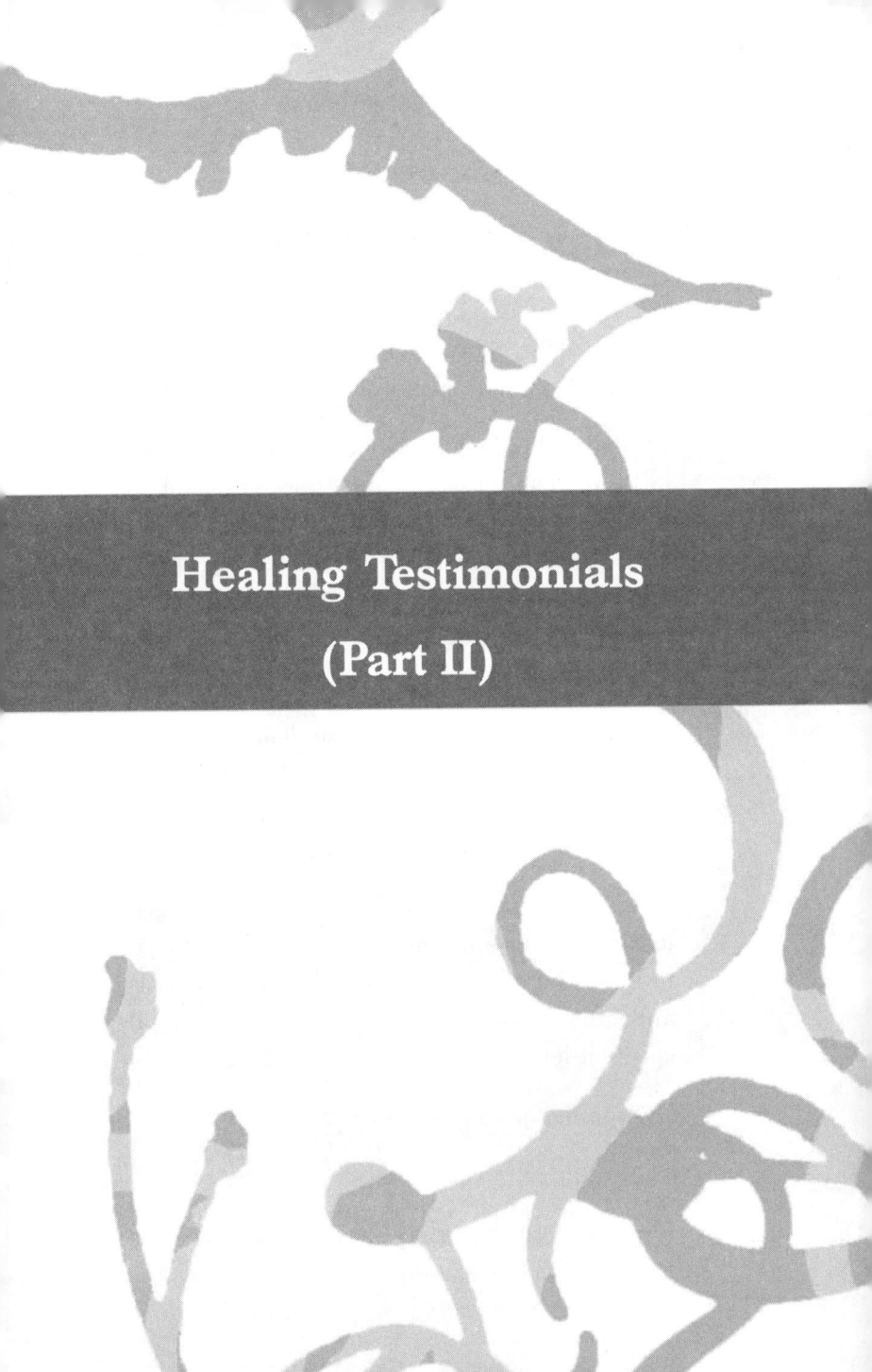

Healing Testimonials
(Part II)

Chapter 12

Healing Testimonials (Part II)

1. With absolute faith, trust and devotion, I went to have *darshan* of Sri Nithyananda Swamiji. I am a 69 year old man having severe pain in both my knees.

   Poojya Sri Swamiji's benevolent look and benediction made me feel reassured and happy. He spoke to me with compassion and concern and touched my left knee for a few minutes. He also touched my chest for a minute and assured me that energy is flowing properly through my *anahata chakra*. I had had an open-heart surgery in May 2002.

   After coming out of the *darshan* hall, the severe pain in my left knee simply vanished. Consequently, I attended healing sessions for about 10 days, which made the pain in my right knee also disappear.

   It was a miracle of Swamiji's divine grace and unconditional compassion for which I am ever grateful to him. I humbly pray to him that he may heal more and more people in the physical, emotional and spiritual levels.

   -H. Varadaraj, Bangalore

   30.01.03

2. It was two years ago that I was diagnosed to be suffering from chronic renal failure. Initially, I was treated as an inpatient at a reputed hospital to bring down my

potassium level, which was very high. I was told, rather curtly, by the doctor that I was born with only one kidney, and the other kidney was also small in size, and functioning below a 25% level, and that it was a gradually deteriorating case.

I was in despair and faithfully followed strict dietary restrictions and medication. In spite of this, the symptoms like vomiting, nausea, breathlessness, etc. were there and I was rushed to a reputed private hospital for emergency treatment. I was administered life-saving medication for a week with dialysis. My agonizing days started thereon with dialysis for three days per week with each session lasting for four hours. Kidney transplantation started haunting me.

I was looking for every conceivable opportunity to get some healing touch. I was referred to the healing powers of Swami Nithyanandaji by a family friend and it was on Thursday, 6th June 2002 that I got an opportunity to attend the healing camp of Swamiji.

I was immensely impressed by the charismatic profile of Swamiji and was convinced of the divine powers of Swamiji. I narrated the nature of my problem and Swamiji just said, 'God's grace is there on you, have courage and you will be healed.' I was mesmerized by his assurance. It was a strange feeling. I felt some heat energy entering my body. I wish to place on record the improvement in my health condition. It was after 5 days of healing, my hemoglobin level, which was precariously low at 6.4g/dl rose to 8.2g/dl and the uric acid reached the normal level of 6mg/dl within the short span of healing. More than anything, I started feeling energetic throughout the day.

-Dr. A.S. Ravindra, Bangalore

3. I met with a major road accident and sustained severe injuries by posterior dislocation of hip, multiple fractures in my left fibula and right tibia.

I had undergone several surgeries on both my legs. I was totally immovable for about 3 years. Thereafter I started to walk with the aid of crutches and a stick. Although my orthopaedic problems were set right, my right leg was still not cured due to swelling and an uncovered ulcer. Plastic surgeries done twice on my right leg were a failure. I was with sorrow and pain, and also having mental agony. With my shortened leg and uncovered ulcer, I was limping, struggling to lead my life and support my family financially as I was the sole bread winner of the family.

One day, I came to know through my relatives about one Swamiji by name of Sri Nithyanandaji and that he was healing all physical and mental ailments and chronic diseases.

I met Swamiji and showed my leg and surrendered my pain and sorrow at his feet when I bowed to him. Immediately Swamiji told me that the ulcer in my leg will be covered with the growth of skin. He asked me to come everyday for the healing sessions. I went regularly to the healing center at Chamundeswari Studio Camp on Cunningham Road.

Firstly, I was relieved of severe pain and stopped taking allopathic painkiller tablets. Secondly, my swollen leg became normal. Thirdly, my limping disappeared. I found it much easier to walk. Moreover, the skin started to cover up my ulcer. Amazingly, my mental agony has gone.

-N.T. Mathivanan, Bangalore

4. I was a diabetic patient. My disease, which I thought was a curse, was in fact a blessing in disguise that was responsible for giving me an opportunity to meet Swamiji. All my family members and I have met Swamiji for different problems, and we have all had improvement after taking healing. He is like a mother who listens to the child's difficulties with love and compassion. He is a doctor to the sick, a Guru to all who seek his blessings and guidance in practical life or spirituality.

-Geetha Krishnan, Bangalore

A Promise to Yourself - Healers' Oaths

Chapter 13
A Promise to Yourself - Healers' Oaths

All discipline should happen with understanding. Be very clear why you are doing what you are doing. When things are very clear, when you understand the rules and regulations, they will not be a burden for you. When you don't understand, it becomes a burden for you. Nothing should be practiced as a rule. Everything should be done by understanding and internalizing.

WHY NO TO DRINKING, SMOKING OR EATING NON-VEGETARIAN FOOD AFTER HEALERS' INITIATION

Why do I say that you should not drink or smoke or eat non-vegetarian food after taking Healers' Initiation? Please be very clear: it is not morality I am trying to impose on you.

When you meditate and practice healing, you will have a beautiful and continuous energy flow. In that high level of energy, if you drink, the low energy alcohol and this high energy of meditation would oppose each other. Indulging in these practices creates a negative energy in the body and by doing *Shakti Dharana* meditation thereafter, it is the negative energy that is awakened.

All these things are a commitment by you to yourself. You have to make it as an understanding and internalization within yourself. I don't want you to suppress yourself. If you can drop smoking or drinking easily, then it is ok.

Otherwise don't take the initiation. Nobody is forcing you to take it. Before taking, think once more if you will be able to do this in a casual way. You should not have to fight with yourself. Do you fight with yourself for drinking poison? No! You know it is not good for you. So also, understand and internalize that drinking, smoking or eating non-vegetarian food will oppose the beautiful energy flow in you that will happen through healing.

Now, let us get into the 3 healing prayer practitioners' oaths. Why is it necessary to take an oath? It is a promise to yourself, to your own consciousness, that's all.

OATH 1

I hereby swear that the healing meditation given to me by Master will be used for the service of all, both animate and inanimate.

We have to understand that nothing is dead on planet earth. Whatever exists is energy. As we saw, this is what the first few words of the Isa Vasya Upanishad say, *'Isa Vasyam Idam Sarvam'* - all that exists is energy. There is nothing like animate or inanimate; what you refer to as inanimate objects merely have lower energy, that's all.

The first oath implies that you will never refuse healing service to anyone or anything in need of it, be they people, animals, plants or inanimate objects. Any personal conflict or difference in ideology with a person should not come in the way of you providing this service to that person.

The healing prayer is an expression of love. Love is the ultimate healing energy. You must have the magnanimity of a good doctor who treats his patients regardless of their status or relationship with him. You may refuse this service to anyone or anything only when your personal life might be in danger.

You should understand your responsibility while taking this oath. This healing service is not yours to give or refuse at your will. The power invested in you flows from a divine source. The Divine does not distinguish between right and wrong or saint and sinner. The Divine's mercy is unconditionally available to all those who ask for it. This gift, this wealth, is not earned by you, but by great people like Patanjali, Jesus and Buddha. Your are therefore not to discriminate as to whom this is to be dispensed to. If you do so, you become a politician. You cannot afford to have enemies now or in the future. You are simply meant to radiate love and compassion. This oath should become a part of your being and your understanding.

COMPASSION FOR EACH AND EVERY ONE

Let me be frank: Spirituality is not practicality in this context. Be very clear that the feeling should be from your heart. You should feel like you are the Mother of planet earth. This healing meditation will work only when your heart melts for one and all in this universe. Keeping hatred in your being will actually harm, disturb or hinder you more than others. You cannot have vengeance against anyone, as it would be a blockage to the energy. This is also a pre-requisite for good health in you.

Understand the meaning of compassion from this small story:

One day, a burglar enters the abode of a master. He requests the master to allow him to spend the night there and the master agrees.

The next morning, the burglar steals the bedroll that he slept on and is about to leave. The master sees him and tells him to take the mat that was beneath the bedroll too. He also tells him that it is customary to thank the giver of any gifts. The surprised burglar thanks the master and runs away.

Later, the office of law apprehends the burglar for his misdeeds and he confesses the various acts of theft he had committed. The office of law asks the master about the theft in his house. The master declares that he himself had gifted his belongings to the burglar and that the burglar had even thanked him for the same. The burglar was simply shaken by what he heard. He just fell at the master's feet and became his disciple.

The healing meditation I am going to give you has been created and perfected over the ages by great masters. It is a culmination of centuries of rigorous *tapas* or penance. The original system was developed by Patanjali. The great spiritual masters who followed him spent their lives in updating and passing this precious gift down through the generations. In order to cherish this legacy and truly be benefited by it, you must be willing to drop your ego and share this gift with joy and compassion.

Remember, the only reason you can have for refusing service would be if the person was likely to violate your person or property. Actually after initiation, you will find that this attitude of compassionate sharing comes upon you naturally. In the presence of this tremendous energy, petty considerations like differences in religion, ideology or personal conflicts simply won't count or have a place in your life anymore.

Drop Your Vengeance and Become Free

Try this exercise:

Let men and women sit separately with a gap in between. Please close your eyes and imagine that your worst enemy is sitting next to you. Try to visualize how you will react when that person is next to you.

(A few minutes pass.)
Relax. Open your eyes.

Now, visualize that the same person has lost his money, his prestige, his power and he has come as a patient to you. There is nobody to take care of him. He comes to you with all his problems. Now, how will you react? Close your eyes and try to visualize.

(A few minutes pass.)
Relax. Open your eyes.

Is there anybody who says, 'Even now I am not able to forgive him?' No!

Actually all our vengeance on others is based on jealousy. You can understand this easily after doing this meditation. When they lose power, position and status, we are ready to forgive them!

Once you learn the technique of dropping vengeance, it will change your whole being. If you do it once, you can and will do it continuously. Your happiness will be with you completely and nobody will be able to make you sad or upset. You will enter into a different space of freedom. It is only when you learn to drop your vengeance that you truly get freedom.

The Healing Touch of Love

Now, who is the single person whom you really love and are close to? It might be your mother or child or spouse or anyone else. Think of that person and close your eyes. Bring to mind all the good things about that person and all the good things the person has done for you. Remember and just be with that person.

Just feel that the person is sitting next to you. Take a few moments to feel the gratitude inside your being and remember the wonderful moments you have had with that person. Cherish those feelings and memories as deeply as possible.

(A few minutes pass.)
Relax. Open your eyes.

Can you see the difference in the two moods: just two minutes ago and now? See how the mood itself has changed! That is the power of love. It can just melt you. Now, if you were to touch anyone in this mood, what would be the effect of such a touch! Just imagine!

It is in this mood that you should provide healing service. Your mood towards him or her will play a significant role. You must be in a loving and compassionate mood when you do the healing meditation. The healing energy will flow tremendously in this mood.

A Promise to Yourself - Healers' Oaths

Practice these four instructions:

1. Take responsibility for the other's suffering.
2. Constantly be with a compassionate and loving feeling as a mother to the whole world.
3. Practice vegetarianism and abstinence from addictives like alcohol and tobacco.
4. Practice *Ananda Gandha*, *Shakti Dharana* and *Nithya Dhyaan* meditations everyday.

Then, a cognitive shift will take place in you and you will move from depression to *ananda* or bliss!

Oath 2

I hereby swear that I will serve regularly and voluntarily at the Nithya Spiritual Healing Centers or start a Healing Center at home.

This oath is to make people responsible.

Understand that Nithya Spiritual Healing is a spiritual service. *Ananda Gandha* is a super-conscious state wherein you will be cheerful and happy during and after the prayer. Besides, it will also kindle your natural intelligence. This is the difference between super-conscious and unconscious energies.

When people heal by unconscious healing methods, you will not feel close to them or go near them comfortably. There will be a certain fear of them. On the other hand, how do you feel during *Ananda Darshan*? Do you ever leave the place of your own accord after having taken *darshan*? No! That is the difference between unconscious and super-conscious healing methods. Do not ever dabble with unconscious healing or healers, as it is dangerous and will enslave you.

Also, remember that this is not an imposition of social service upon you. It is purely your choice. Healing meditation is simply a process of connecting individual intelligence to cosmic intelligence and helping drop social conditioning to express our true nature, which is bliss.

To be an instrument in this process, you need to first drop your own conditioning - the ideas about yourself. That can only happen when you make an honest commitment to fall in tune with your own dimension, by working out my teachings in your life in an honest way.

Are you totally willing to transform your own life? Are you ready to become more loving, gentler and more compassionate? Remember, I don't want you to just spread my word, I want you to practice it. Unless you bring about a transformation in your own life, how will you reach out to others?

OATH 3

I hereby swear that I will follow all the rules existing at present and updated or amended in future by Master and His institution.

Yes, this is a self-explanatory oath.

SIGNIFICANCE OF THE HOMA RITUAL

We will now perform a *homa* or fire ritual to Lord *Anandeshwara*.

Let us first of all understand what a fire ritual or *homa* is. Whether you believe it or not, accept it or not, you are from the five elements - earth, water, fire, air and space.

The divine energy or the energy of Existence is available to us in the form of space. With the *bimba* or by idol worship, we harness energy through the earth element. With the *kalasha*, or by bathing in holy waters, we harness energy through the water element. When we perform fire rituals or *homa*, we harness energy through the fire element. When we chant *mantras*, we harness that energy through the air element.

Now we are going to worship the 'Shiva energy' through fire. We are going to thank Shiva for everything that He has given us. To achieve and constantly be in the state of Shiva consciousness, we are now going to perform this *homa* to Lord *Anandeshwara*.

ANANDA GANDHA INITIATION

You may come one by one to me. I will be touching your *ajna chakra*. There might be a piercing or tingling sensation in the area between your *anahata* and *manipuraka chakras* at that moment. Do not fear; just relax. After that, we will be doing the *Ananda Gandha* meditation.

Master initiates each one present.

(After the initiation)

Each one of you has successfully taken the initiation!

Healing Testimonials (Part III)

Chapter 14
Healing Testimonials (Part III)

1. I happened to read an article published in the Hindu newspaper about Swamiji's healing powers, and I also came to know more about Him through my neighbor. I had been suffering from certain health problems. I went to meet *Swamiji* at His Bangalore City center. For a few days I used to just stand and watch Him healing others. One day as I stood in the queue for His *darshan*, I could feel warmth right from my heart welcoming me into His divine grace. That's when I realized that there is much more to *Swamiji* than His physical form.

   I had been suffering from backache, throat infection and headache for several years. I decided to take healing from *Swamiji*. During the first healing done by *Swamiji*, these symptoms reduced by 50%. After the complete 15 sessions of healing, my problems disappeared completely. I was further advised to attend the Ananda Spurana Program at Devanahalli, which *Swamiji* himself conducted. It was a great opportunity and unique experience to learn various meditation techniques and spend two whole days in the presence of this great enlightened Master. I came back from the program, a totally transformed person with a very positive frame of mind and feeling blissful. Since then there has been no turning back.

   After being healed and attending the first ASP, I wanted to become a healer. I was asked to attend another ASP.

After the second ASP, I came back feeling totally rejuvenated and felt as though I was transported to another world. I was feeling a joy that is beyond any worldly description.

On June 29th 2003, I was initiated to be a healer by Swamiji and started a healing center at my home. Since then I have been doing healing for people with different ailments. It is a wonderful experience being a channel of Swamiji in the healing process. The flow of the divine energy through me gives me totally new vitality and vigor. These days there is not a dull moment in my life. Any symptoms of any kind of problem, physical, mental or otherwise that I face, disappear as I carry out Swamiji's healing. With love and devotion I totally surrender at the lotus feet of this Divine Master.

-Viji Shankar, Bangalore

2. In 2004 I had just completed my Nithya Spiritual Healing initiation. My daughter was a year and a half old, having severe fever up to 102 degrees F. I told my wife not to panic, and asked her to put the child on her lap and sit near me. I started healing by praying to Swamiji. Within 10 minutes, the child recovered from fever and started having milk.

-D.S. Madhavan, Bangalore

3. Nithyanandam! I am a Healer in Arizona, US.

This past summer I was at a dear friend's house for a birthday party (for her husband). She was limping around with a temporary brace on her knee, fixing food, chasing her triplets who were less than a year-old, and busily hosting this get-together. I had heard about her injury the week before, but now was witnessing her hopping around, trying to keep weight off her hurt knee.

Earlier that week she had been carrying one of her tots from the bedroom to the kitchen, which entailed stepping over a baby gate. As she stepped over the gate her toe caught the top and she began to fall forward with baby in arms. As she was falling she knew she would have to sacrifice her body in order to keep the baby in her arms safely. So down she went, landing directly on her bent knee on the hard tile floor, with baby in arms and with no way to slow her fall with her own hands. The baby was unharmed, but my friend suffered badly from the impact on her knee.

All that week she had been icing her knee, resting it as much as she could, and doing what she knew best to heal it. She had told me that she could not straighten it without excruciating pain, and also could not bend it fully. As the party came to an end, I asked if I could do a healing session for her. She happily found the couch and relaxed into a comfortable lying-down position. She said she had an appointment the next day to get a X-ray and diagnosis from a doctor. I went into *Ananda Gandha*, laid my hands on her knee for about 10 minutes and then said my goodbyes to her and her family.

The next morning at around 7:00 a.m. the phone at my home rang. She was on the line saying, 'I don't know what you did to me, but my knee is completely healed! I can walk on it, straighten it, bend it fully...all without pain! Thank you! Thank you!' Chills ran up my spine, 'It wasn't me!' I said.

-Ma Nithyananda Nischala (Cassandra Wallick), Phoenix, AZ, USA

4. Yesterday a man from Auckland asked to have a healing here in Rotorua, now a center for New Zealand. His whole hip was disintegrated (he saw from the latest MRI) from a boat accident 12 years ago. He walked in using a cane and in pain. I seated him in front of Swamiji's photo and placed my hands on his crown and *anahata chakra*. After 5 or 7 minutes I completed the healing and left the room. He remained seated in front of Swamiji's photo listening to the mantras for several minutes. When I returned he got up from the chair and walked. He said his whole hip had opened and he had no pain. He asked for a meditation he could do at home. He gratefully took with him the Nithya Dhyaan meditation CD and the audio of Guaranteed Solutions.

-Ma Kalaadevi, New Zealand

Spiritual Name

Chapter 15

Spiritual Name

WHAT IS IN A NAME?

When somebody calls out, 'John' or 'Jill', immediately, unconsciously, the attention of John or Jill is drawn and the person looks to see who is calling him or her. This is how deeply our name has been embedded in our unconscious. Your name can be a powerful technique for realizing yourself.

Another important thing is that whenever someone calls out your name, you suddenly become conscious and aware of yourself. You must have experienced a situation such as sitting in a big classroom and suddenly, the teacher calls out your name for some reason. Whether you were dozing off or listening to the teacher, you will break from that thought pattern, and you will be jolted to the present place and time.

SIGNIFICANCE OF THE SPIRITUAL NAME

The new name which I give, this spiritual name, is to constantly remind you to mother the psychological revolution which has happened in you. You constantly mother the new life, the new understanding which has happened in you. Constantly you remember it. That is why I give you the new name.

A name has a tremendous influence over our state of mind. The spiritual name indicates the spiritual path of the individual according to his or her innate nature, which will lead to the ultimate flowering of the individual and actualization of his or her potential.

Spiritual Name

When we call out the person's name, his or her spiritual path is constantly repeated and it enters into the very core of his or her being. When a psychological revolution happens inside you, again and again if you remember the old name, you go back to the old identity.

If you have the right spiritual name given by an enlightened being, that name will take you to conscious depths. It will be a bridge for you to enter into enlightenment. It will direct you in your path towards enlightenment. It will tell you how your way of life should be, how you can achieve enlightenment and how you should take care of your life.

There are thousands of ways to live. To give you guidance, masters choose the name. Your name is like a *mantra*.

Let me give the definition of *samskara* and *mantra*. Any word which is inscribed in your inner space which binds you, which suffocates you, which brings you down in your consciousness is *samskara*, an engram.

Any word that is inscribed in your inner space, which liberates you, which takes you to a higher consciousness, which takes you to the more joyful, blissful state is *mantra*.

Mantra and *samskara* both are almost the same, but *samskara* binds you. *Mantra* liberates you. *Mantra* is the antidote for *samskara*.

If you are named by an unconscious person, your name is a bondage. If you are named by an enlightened being, your name is a method to liberate you. Your very name can be used as a technique for enlightenment.

You see, if at all your name can be used towards your spiritual growth, that is the best thing, because the whole day from morning till night, either you will be using it for yourself or somebody else will be using that name for you. Then understand, every moment becomes a spiritual practice. If the right word from the right master is given to you as a technique, as a name, every time it is repeated, you are entering into the higher consciousness. Every time you understand and remember the meaning of it, you are in a different plane.

People come and tell me, 'The spiritual name you gave me is so beautiful. Whenever I remember that name, I am fulfilled. Whenever I meditate on its meaning, I am just overflowing.' The name can take you to the deepest level.

One more thing, any other word is only an addition to you, but your name is the center of you. Your name is the center, everything else is an addition. That is why in the *vedic* tradition we use only some god's name. We have, for every god, 1008 names, *sahasranama*. *Sahasranama* is used for two different purposes. One is to address the gods and deities; the other is to pick up names for your kids. Our elders would try to find the appropriate name. They would see the family deity and the *nakshatra* of the child and refer to the *sahasranama* to find out the right name. The name is so powerful, it can take you beyond the mind.

To be a Nithya Spiritual Healer, you are required to change your name legally to your spiritual name given by Paramahamsa.

Nithya Spiritual Healing
In Practice

Chapter 16
Nithya Spiritual Healing In Practice

The uniqueness of the Nithya Spiritual Healing technique is that, it not only helps the person you are healing but also helps in your own spiritual growth.

For social reasons, you can directly touch and heal only people of your gender. For the opposite gender, please use the healing stick provided to you during the Nithya Spiritual Healers' Initiation.

Nithya Spiritual Healing Technique

1. Place your palms on the pertinent chakra of the person being healed. The healer's chart below and the location of the *chakras* (Figure 3) will guide you about which *chakra* is related to which disease and how to heal the relevant *chakra*.

2. Close your eyes and visualize my laughing face. This is the key that will unlock the whole process initially.

3. Immediately you will find energy gushing forth from your *Ananda Gandha chakra*. Move deeply inwards and try to discover the source of this energy. Simply relax into yourself. Don't worry about the energy flow; it will happen on its own.

Nithya Spiritual Healing in Practice

4. Once you have relaxed into yourself, drop my laughing face and feel only the boundless energy.

5. Continue as long as you feel the person is drawing the energy. You will sense this effortlessly. Your hands will automatically drop once the person has had enough.

Healer's Chart

Disease	Chakras to be healed
Ordinary fever	Anahata
High fever	Sahasrara, Anahata
Headache, Migraine	Sahasrara; spot healing
Diabetes	Anahata
Hypertension	Anahata
Skin diseases	Muladhara, Sahasrara, soles of feet (apply energized ash or *vibhuti* on the soles of the feet)
Arthritis	Muladhara, back of neck
Anemia	Sahasrara, Anahata
Getting over alcohol and smoking habits	Swadishtana, energized honey
Cancer	Swadishtana, Muladhara, spot healing

Kidney trouble	On the back where the kidneys are located
Uterus problems, menstrual disorders	Muladhara
Bed wetting	Muladhara
Insomnia	Vishuddhi
Eye problems	Ajna, eyes
Stomach problems, ulcer, diarrhea, vomiting	Manipuraka, Muladhara
ENT problems	Vishuddhi, spot healing
Respiratory problems	Vishuddhi, Anahata
Nose bleeding	Ajna
Heart diseases	Anahata
Nervous disorders, rheumatism, numbness	Sahasrara
Epilepsy	Sahasrara, Anahata
Coma	Sahasrara
Paralysis	Muladhara, back of neck
Stress	Manipuraka, Anahata
Sprains and fractures	Vishuddhi, spot healing
Improvement of overall immunity	Vishuddhi, Anahata

Nithya Spiritual Healing in Practice

Giddiness	Sahasrara, Anahata
Obesity, underweight	Manipuraka
Sinus disorders, common cold	Vishuddhi, Anahata
Tuberculosis	Vishuddhi, Anahata
Jaundice	Manipuraka, Anahata
Constipation	Manipuraka
Piles	Muladhara
Hernia	Swadishtana, Muladhara
Toothache	Spot healing
Stammering, Speech difficulties	Sahasrara, energized honey
Low back pain	Muladhara, spot healing
Disorders associated with blood	Sahasrara
All types of fear	Swadishtana, Anahata
Multiple sclerosis	Anahata, back of neck
Alzheimer's disease	Sahasrara
Parkinson's disease	Sahasrara, left arm

If you are not sure as to which chakra to place your hands or the healing stick on during the healing service, simply direct the energy to *anahata* and *sahasrara* chakras.

Etiquette for Nithya Spiritual Healers

- Have a smiling face.
- Let your body language show care and concern.
- Empathize.
- Radiate warmth and peace.
- Be in and with Nithyananda - eternal bliss.
- Keep your ego aside. You are channels of Nithyananda.
- Maintain silence within the spiritual healing area and ensure others maintain silence too.
- Be aware and sensitive to the needs of those around you.
- Create a warm network with your colleagues. You are creating a family.
- As far as possible, male spiritual healers will attend to men and female spiritual healers will attend to women.
- If you are healing a person of the opposite gender, use the healing stick provided to you at the time of Healers' Initiation.
- Play Nithya *kirtans* during the healing prayer service.
- Give priority to mothers with infants, expectant mothers, senior citizens and physically challenged people.

- Do not favor friends and relatives.

- Unaccompanied ladies should be given preference at night time for reasons of safety.

- Strictly abstain from alcohol, smoking and non-vegetarian food. Avoid onions, green chilies, garlic, and stimulants like coffee and tea.

- Do *Shakti Dharana* meditation every night before going to sleep. Do *Ananda Gandha* meditation everyday for at least 21 minutes. Do *Nithya Dhyaan* meditation everyday.

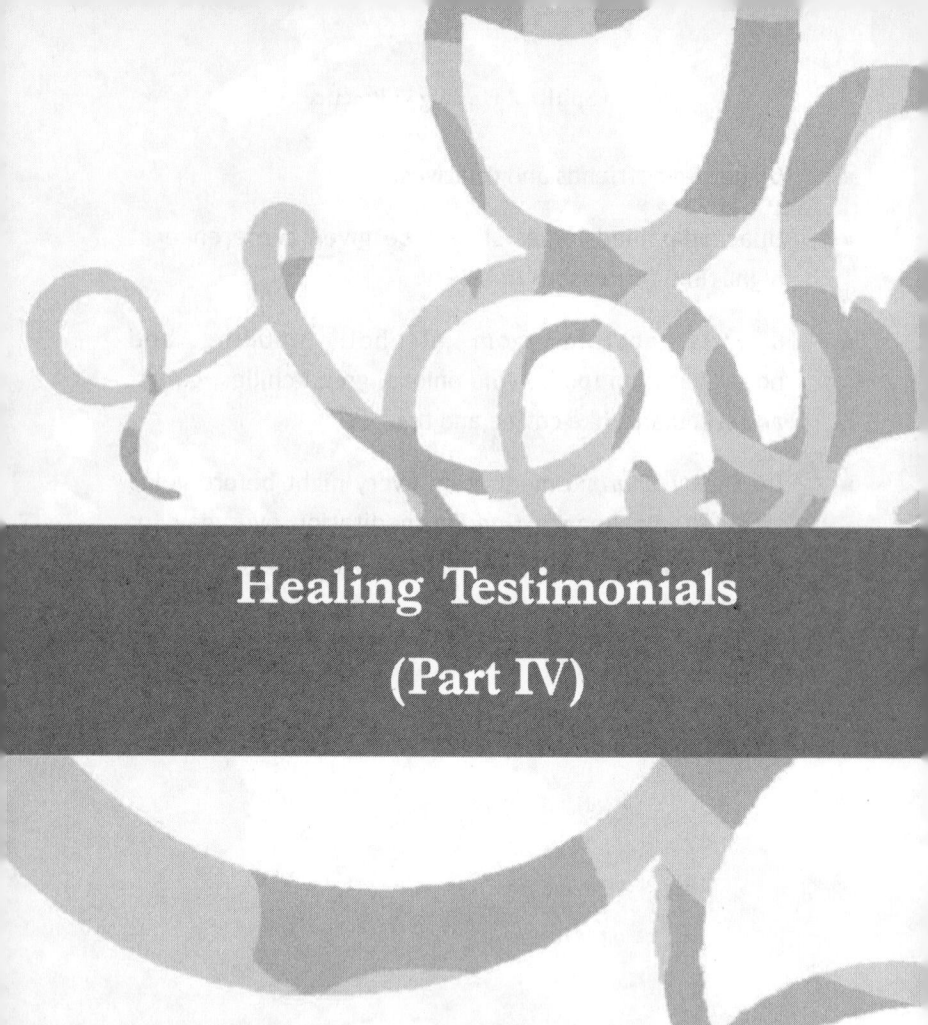

Healing Testimonials
(Part IV)

Chapter 17
Healing Testimonials (Part IV)

1. A few days ago I had a sore throat. Swallowing was painful. In the evening I did self-healing. The next morning it was almost gone. So I did self-healing again. A few hours later I remembered that I had a sore throat earlier but the pain was totally gone and there was no more pain ever since. Wow! Was I glad because a sore throat usually means big trouble for me. And this is actually the second time it beautifully healed. The same had happened a few months back.
   -Ma Nithyananda Udaysree

2. I had returned from a trip to the Bidadi ashram and my friends were curious to hear all about the various meditation programs I had attended. I told about all the programs I had done in the ashram, including Healers' Initiation. The audience, a mixture of Indians and Americans found the idea of healing interesting and fascinating and looked at me with a bit of disbelief. After our discussion, one of my American friends came to me and said she was going through chronic anxiety and suffering frequently from 'anxiety attacks'. She wondered if the healing would work on mental problems also, or if they were just for physical issues. I explained to her that the healing energy is intelligence and it works at all levels. I told her that it would help with mental problems like anxiety and

depression much more than purely physical problems. So she was interested in trying it out. I healed her for about 15 minutes before she left for her home. She called me the next day and thanked me sincerely. She said she felt such a deep sense of peace and relaxation during and after the healing that she slept exceptionally well that night. She also mentioned that she hadn't slept that well in 4 years, when a major incident in her life had become the source of all her anxiety ever since.

-Ma Nithyananda Premeshwari Mayi

3. Last year, my uncle and aunt were visiting us in Singapore. During their stay here, they made a short trip to Tioman islands in Malaysia. When they returned home, both of them were in really bad shape. Apparently, they had a bad experience with the sea, which almost drowned them while snorkeling. They had swallowed huge amounts of sea water and were still in a state of shock when they returned. My uncle was in shivering fits and was running a high temperature. I just asked him to lie down and relax. I took Swami's name and started giving healing on his *sahasrara* and *anahata*. After about 10 minutes he drifted off into deep sleep. The next morning when he woke up, he was so perfectly back to normal, as though nothing had happened at all!

-Sri Nithyananda Arpana

4. A middle aged lady heard about Swami and healing through her tenant. She had serious health

complications and had undergone several major surgeries, the recent one being a few months ago. Starting from chest pain to stomach pain to back pain to knee pain...She started coming to my home regularly for healing, almost thrice a week. After a few weeks of healing, when she did her medical check up, she said the doctors gave her very positive feedback in terms of her recovery. Her blood pressure and sugar had touched almost normal. She is very grateful to Swamiji and is now planning to attend LBP.

-Ma Nithyananda Arpana

5. Just before we inaugurated our Life Bliss center in Singapore last year in October, we were busy setting up all items necessary for our activities. We had just purchased a TV. Although second-hand, it was hardly used, and was in perfect working condition. We had checked it many times before we bought it. Now after cleaning up and setting up the center, we thought let us celebrate by playing a video of Swamiji. When we tried to switch it on, all we heard was a very high-pitched noise and a badly blurred image on screen. It was terrible. The volunteer who transported the TV to our center said, 'While in the taxi, it was subject to some jerks and bumps, so maybe we need to get a service person or replace it.' We said 'No, before that, we are going to give healing.' So two of us healers laid our hands on the TV lovingly and started giving healing. Wonder of wonders, after about 5 minutes the noise gradually subsided. We

then switched off the TV and then switched it on to double check: No noisy sound and a perfect image on screen. The TV is still in perfect condition at our center now!

-Ma Nithyananda Arpana

6. Last week, I started to develop an eye infection. What started off as a mild pain on my left eye in the morning had developed into a boil and left the eye sockets swollen by the end of the day. I went back home and remembered the *vibhuti* (holy ash) that Swamiji had given during blessings this time at Jayanti. I just mixed the *vibhuti* with water, closed my eyes and applied it all over, telling myself that I will be perfectly fine by next morning. And the next morning, I tried searching for the boil but couldn't spot it! It was amazing.

Apart from this, personally, I cannot even remember the number of times *Ananda Gandha* has helped me recover. I used to have severe pain during periods and a severe migraine problem. Taking a paracetamol was a weekly (if not daily) ritual. Now, honestly, I have not touched a painkiller in the last 2 years.

-Ma Nithyananda Arpana

7. I had been suffering from chronic lower back pain (~50% of the time) since 2000. I had tried chiropractors, yoga, tai-chi, weight lifting, etc. but I did not get much relief. The 2-day ATSP program in May 2007 appeared to make my back pain worse as I was not used to sitting for extensive periods.

However, within a few minutes after the *energy darshan*, I noticed that my low back pain was completely gone. Ever since, my lower back pain has been sporadic (less than 5%). Occasionally when I do have lower back pain, I notice that it is completely healable with self-healing meditation. The pain heals within a few days while in the past each event would last several weeks or months.

-Nithya Nayakan

Chakra Counseling

Chapter 18
Chakra Counseling

The Nithya Spiritual Healer can offer *chakra* counseling during the healing session as well. Each of the *chakras* is associated with certain emotions and gets locked by certain emotions while the corresponding positive emotion results in the *chakra* healing.

Chakra	Blocked by	Healed by
Muladhara	**Fantasy**, lust, greed	Welcoming reality
Swadishtana	**Fear**, phobia	Facing fear
Manipuraka	**Worry**	Drop worrying about worry
Anahata	**Attention need**, expectation	Love, acceptance, compassion
Vishuddhi	**Jealousy**	Realizing one's uniqueness
Ajna	**Ego**, seriousness	Simplicity
Sahasrara	**Discontentment**	Gratitude

Table 1: Chakras and Emotions

We have to understand that the majority of people around the world are caught in the lower four *chakras* - *muladhara*, *swadishtana*, *manipuraka* and *anahata*. If we analyze further, the Western mind is more caught in problems relating to the *muladhara* chakra while the Eastern mind is usually caught in *anahata* chakra-based problems. The *manipuraka* and *swadishtana* related problems are common, whether it is the Western mind or the Eastern mind.

CLASSIFICATION OF *Chakras*

We can classify the various *chakras* as predominantly male or female based on which get commonly affected in men and women.

Lower 4 chakras:

Muladhara - male

Swadishtana - female

Manipuraka - male

Anahata -female

Higher 3 chakras:

Vishuddhi - female

Ajna - Ardhanareeshwara (realizing both the male and female halves in oneself)

Sahasrara - Beyond the differences and limitations of gender

Based on the guideline chart (Table 1), we can diagnose for any person what *chakra* his problem is related to. Once we diagnose this, the solution can be given as a complement to healing. This ensures that the mental setup which is the root cause of the disease is changed.

SAME CHAKRA SOLUTION

The immediate solution for the diseased *chakra* is to give the person the basic understanding about how that *chakra* works, how it gets blocked and how it can be energized.

COMPLEMENTARY *Chakra* SOLUTION

The understanding of the complementary chakra (the opposite gender *chakra* next to the diseased *chakra*) and the meditation can be given. This is because the *chakra* under consideration is low on energy. So, we are using the complementary *chakra* to provide the energy needed. The complementary *chakra* pairs are *muladhara-swadishtana*, *manipuraka-anahata* and *vishuddhi-ajna*.

For example, if the problem is relating to *muladhara chakra*, the follow-up can be about the complementary chakra, the *swadishtana chakra*. The problem is related to fantasy; the solution is related to courage. The person is in his fantasy world because he feels he doesn't have the means to realize what he wants in reality. He can be given the powerful secret of life - the power of *iccha shakti* (power of desire).

LIFE SOLUTION

The life solution for holistic health of the person is to recommend doing the Life Bliss Program Level 1 - ASP which will give an in-depth understanding about the *chakras*. This can then lead up to the Nithya Spiritual Healing Initiation so that the person now knows how to constantly be in a state of bliss - *Ananda Gandha*.

Guidelines for Nithya Spiritual Healing

Chapter 19

Guidelines for Nithya Spiritual Healing
(Legal Guidelines)

1. Understand and acknowledge that the practice of Nithya Spiritual Healing is a religious and spiritual prayer and meditation service only. It does not involve the diagnosis or treatment of any medical or psychological conditions and does not involve the use of any physical intervention or manipulation of the human body. Any benefit that an individual experiences comes from within himself or herself, based on his or her body's ability to heal on its own.

2. Do not make any guarantees, warranties, or representations regarding the outcome of the Nithya Spiritual Healing process, and specifically do not claim that the process in any way diagnoses, treats, heals, cures or prevents any disease, illness, injury, or physical or mental condition.

3. Do not use the word 'patient' to describe someone who elects to receive your Nithya Spiritual Healing services.

4. If you are a licensed physician or other licensed health care practitioner, advise everyone to whom you are provide Nithya Spiritual Healing services that such services do not constitute diagnosis, care or treatment or the practice of medicine or any other health care

Nithya Spiritual Healing

technology. Further, do not engage or claim to engage in medical diagnosis, care or treatment or in the practice of medicine or any other health care profession in conjunction with any of your activities as a Nithya Spiritual Healing Practitioner.

5. Collect and maintain on file duly executed forms, consenting to the services you perform as a Nithya Spiritual Healing practitioner and releasing yourself, Nithyananda Mission, Nithyananda Dhyanapeetam, Life Bliss Foundation, and Paramahamsa Nithyananda from liability arising from the services. Consult an attorney to ensure that the forms are appropriate, given the laws applicable in the areas where you will be providing services. Be aware that such laws may change from time to time.

6. Understand and acknowledge that your participation in the Nithya Spiritual Healing program is on a voluntary basis. Do not charge, or accept any fees for Nithya Spiritual Healing services that you may provide to others.

7. Understand and acknowledge that you, as an individual practitioner, are responsible for any Nithya Spiritual Healing services you provide. Paramahamsa Nithyananda, Nithyananda Mission, Nithyananda Dhyanapeetam, Life Bliss Foundation or any sister organizations thereof are not responsible, or liable for any consequences, claims or damages, direct or indirect, arising from the spiritual healing services that you provide to other individuals.

Guidelines for Nithya Spiritual Healing

8. Do not provide Nithya Spiritual Healing services if you are suffering from any physical, mental or psychological disorders or taking any medicines for any physical, mental or psychological disorders.

9. If you become aware that an individual who has requested your Nithya Spiritual Healing services appears to suffer from a mental disorder, do not provide Nithya Spiritual Healing services and recommend that he or she seek attention from an appropriate licensed health care practitioner or mental health care provider.

10. Nithyananda Mission, Nithyananda Dhyanapeetam and Life Bliss Foundation reserve the right to make amendments or changes to the Nithya Spiritual Healing guidelines from time to time. The practitioner agrees to adhere to any such changes in the guidelines published by Nithyananda Mission, Nithyananda Dhyanapeetam and Life Bliss Foundation and also agrees periodically to visit the official website of Nithyananda Dhyanapeetam to update himself or herself with respect to any changes.

11. Nithya Spiritual Healing guidelines are available online at:http://www.dhyanapeetam.org/Web/aghealguidelines.asp

Surya Namaskar

Chapter 20
Surya Namaskar
Eternal Sun salutation

Surya Namaskar is part of Nithya Yoga – an understanding of Yoga gifted to humanity by Nithyananda. The uniqueness of Nithya Yoga is that it directly brings to life the original teachings of Patanjali by adapting it to suit the modern mind. Sage Patanjali, from southern India, is considered to be the Father of Yoga.

Surya Namaskar is a daily salutation to the Sun. Not only does it help keep the body at peak functioning, it also brings a complete awareness of the body-mind connection.

> Everything is yoga! Everything can become Yoga. If everything becomes Yoga, only then you are in eternal Yoga - Nithya Yoga.
>
> - Paramahamsa Nithyananda
> Introduction to Nithya Yoga
> January 2007, Bidadi ashram

BENEFITS OF SURYA NAMASKAR

The practice of Surya Namaskar awakens the body intelligence to directly draw energy from the Sun. Surya Namaskar is designed to access the etheric energy around us. When practiced facing the East in the first rays of the morning sun along with the appropriate breathing technique and the corresponding (appropriate) *mantras* (chants), it has tremendous effect on the mind, body and spirit. Nothing more needs to be done.

Surya Namaskar works on all body parts, every organ, system and *chakra* (vital energy center in the body). It is a sequence of postures done dynamically with the appropriate breathing.

Every morning, you may do six to twelve repetitions of Surya Namaskar (Sun Salutation). Of all the yogic postures, Surya Namaskar is considered the most effective way to limber up, tone, stretch and strengthen the entire body and spine. Surya Namaskar is regarded as the king of all postures.

Significance of Surya Namaskar *Mantras*

A *mantra* (chant) is a composition of syllables, words, phrases or sentences that when repeated with awareness has a very powerful and penetrating influence on the mind. The Surya Namaskar *mantra* comprises a *bija* (seed) *mantra* and a glorification *mantra*. The glorification is of the Sun God.

The *bija* (seed) *mantra* has no meaning by itself but the vibration of it in the human system is very powerful. The 'Theory of Vibration' as expounded by modern scientists, was put to direct application thousands of years ago by the ancient inner world scientists - our *vedic* seers!

Scientific studies conducted by Dr. Masaru Emoto of Japan have clearly proven that the vibration of sound has a profound effect on water. Considering that the human body is more than 80% water, it is evident how much sound vibrations can influence our system. Unconscious thoughts and emotions create strong vibrations within us in the form of stored memories or samskaras. We need to dissolve them with awareness and create a completely positive consciousness.

There are six *bija mantras* and they are:

Om hraam

Om hreem

Om hroom

Om hraim

Om hraum

Om hraha

The glorification *mantras* highlight the glorious qualities of the Sun. Each *mantra* is chanted with complete awareness before every round of Surya Namaskar. The *mantra* is empowered to confer the same qualities on the committed practitioner.

Through these simple set of steps, we can realize that the outer Sun symbolizes the shining intelligence of our inner self. We come to understand our connection to the cosmic energy that is all-pervasive.

Surya Namaskar *mantras* (formed by combining the *bija mantras* with the glorification *mantras*)

1. ~ om hraam mitraaya namaha
   Salutations to the eternal friend of all

2. ~om hreem ravaye namaha
   Salutations to the eternal shining one

3. ~om hroom suryaaya namaha
   Salutations to the eternal one who induces activity

4. ~ om hraim bhaanave namaha
   Salutations to the eternal one who illumines

5. ~ om hraum khagaaya namaha
   Salutations to the eternal one who moves swiftly

6. ~ om hraha pushne namaha
   Salutations to the eternal giver of strength

7. ~ om hraam hiranya garbhaya namaha
   Salutations to the eternal golden cosmic womb

8. ~om hreem mareechaye namaha
   Salutations to the eternal Lord of dawn

9. ~ om hroom adityaaya namaha
   Salutations to the eternal son of Aditi, the infinite cosmic mother

10. ~ om hraim saavitre namaha
    Salutations to the eternal benevolent mother

11. ~ om hraum arkaaya namaha
    Salutations to the eternal one who is praiseworthy

12. ~ om hraha bhaaskaraaya namaha
    Salutations to the eternal one who leads to enlightenment

Figure 13 : Surya Nakaskar Mantras

Breathe In Suffering, Breathe Out Bliss

In Surya Namaskar, every motion is synchronized with the breath. As a Nithya Spiritual Healer, you can not only do a great service to yourself but to the whole of planet earth by doing Surya Namaskar everyday.

With every breath you take in, visualize clearly you are inhaling the suffering and negativity from the world. You are reducing the collective negativity. Now, when the breath, the *prana*, goes inside your body, *Ananda Gandha*, the source of energy, will simply transform it into your very nature of bliss. You have the power to transform suffering into bliss because you are in touch with the very source of energy. When you exhale, exhale the bliss. Actively contribute to the collective positivity in the universe.

Asana Sequence of Surya Namaskar

This should be done on an empty stomach preferably in the morning.

Asana (Posture) Sequence of Surya Namaskar

1. Stand with the feet slightly apart for balance. Bring the hands together into *namaskar* (prayer position) in front of the chest. Keep the eyes open throughout the practice of Surya Namaskar. Chant the corresponding Surya Namaskar *mantra* (refer chart).

2. Inhaling, gracefully sweep the arms up over your head and gently arch the spine backwards.

Nithya Spiritual Healing

1   2   3

3. Exhaling, sweep the arms forward and down so the hands touch the floor either side of the feet and close to them, and the forehead comes in close to the knees. Please bend the knees to allow for greater ease in doing this.

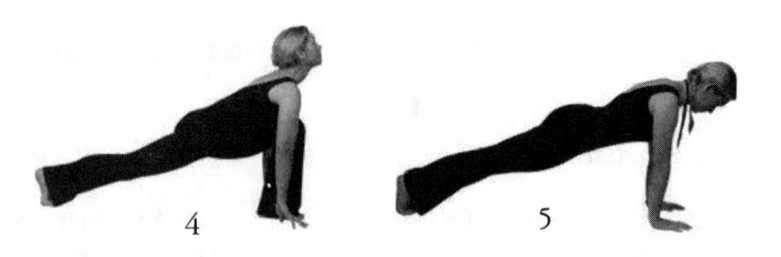

4   5

4. Inhaling, step the right foot back as far as you can and lift your heart center up, looking up at the same time.

5. Holding the breath, step the left foot back and come into a plank position with the spine, neck and head in one

Surya Namaskar

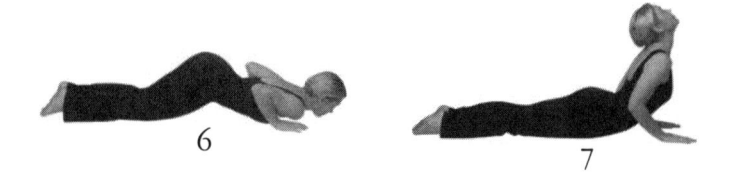

straight line, your hands placed directly beneath your shoulders and eyes looking down at the floor.

6. On the exhale, lower the knees, chest, and chin to the floor and assume *ashtanga namaskara* (salute with eight parts or points touching the floor). Let your stomach be off the floor with your hips lifted up gently, the elbows tucked in.

7. On the inhale, point the toes out, relax your stomach to touch the floor, keep the elbows bent at a 90 degree angle and gently push with your hands and lift the chest off the floor. Come into *bhujangasana* (cobra pose).

8. On the exhale, push with your hands, raise your hips upwards and backwards into the air and assume *bhujangasana* (downward facing dog pose). Spread the fingers wide and gently push your heels toward the floor.

179

Nithya Spiritual Healing

If you are unable to touch the floor with your heels, don't bother about it. But don't shift your position in order for them to touch.

9. With a soft gaze look forward between your hands and step the right foot forward as far as you can, between the hands and in line with them if possible. Inhale, lifting your chin and chest.

10. Step the left foot forward to meet the right foot. Bend your knees slightly if you need to. Exhale and bring the head in close to the legs.

11. On the inhale, sweep your arms up over your head and gently arch the spine saluting the Sun.

12. Exhale, bring your arms down, and your hands back into prayer position in front of your heart.

Repeat the Surya Namaskar for at least 6 rounds, each time alternating between the right and left leg in steps 4 and 9.

Ashtanga Yoga - the Eightfold Path to Bliss for the Healer

1. Laughing meditation

Laughter is a wonderful meditation technique. The technique of the ancient Zen tradition of masters and disciples is to touch no-mind through laughter.

As soon as you wake up in the morning, even before you get up from your bed, laugh for five minutes! Just laugh at yourself. Laugh without a reason!

Laughter is known to heal a number of diseases, especially diseases related to the nervous system and throat. A hearty laugh is said to squeeze out harmful byproducts of cellular functioning.

2. Oil-pulling

Before brushing your teeth, eating or drinking anything, take 1 full tablespoon of either sesame or refined sunflower oil. Put it in your mouth, sit in one place, tilt your chin up so that the oil gets to the back molar teeth, and slowly pull through your softly gritted teeth for 15 - 20 minutes. Don't multitask while doing this. At the end of it, spit the oil out in the toilet and brush your teeth well. If you have pulled properly, the oil that you spit out will be thin, whitish colour water. Drink 2 glasses of water after this cleaning of the mouth,

Note: Do not swallow the oil that you pull. It will contain parasites and bacteria.

If you have to pull oil after meals, wait at least 4 hours before you do it.

Oil pulling is said to benefit anything from cracked heels to cancer. Exhaustive research reports on the benefits of oil pulling are available on the web for reading.

3. Ananda Gandha meditation and Nithya Dhyaan

Do *Ananda Gandha* meditation for at least 21 minutes everyday. Do Nithya Dhyaan meditation everyday. (www.lifeblissmeditation.org)

4. Surya Namaskar

Do at least 12 rounds of Surya Namaskar everyday in the morning.

5. **Remain in Ananda Gandha as much as possible**

    Whenever you remember, go into *Ananda Gandha*. Do every activity, simple or complex, while being in *Ananda Gandha*.

6. **At least for half an hour everyday, read a book, or hear a discourse of Paramahamsa Nithyananda.**

7. **Connect to the Master everyday from 7 pm to 7:20 pm.**

    The time from 7 pm to 7:20 pm is the time when Paramahamsa is available directly to all his devotees. Share this wonderful gift of the presence of the Master with one and all. Do healing, conduct *satsangs* in your healing center.

8. **At night, before going to bed, do Shakti Dharana meditation everyday.**

Your Questions Answered

Chapter 21

Your Questions Answered

Q. What happens if I put my hands or healing stick on the wrong chakra *unknowingly?*

With Nithya Spiritual Healing, there will be no negative side effects. If the energy flows to the wrong *chakra*, the benefit may be a little delayed, that's all. But eventually it will help because all the *chakras* are connected.

Q. Can I do healing service for myself?

Yes, you can. Nithya Spiritual Healing is actually a meditation technique. So, when you meditate, the energy flows inside you and heals you.

Q. Can I initiate others into becoming Nithya Spiritual Healers?

No. Only Paramahamsa can do the initiation.

Q. Can I teach Ananda Gandha meditation to others?

No. The meditation itself can be practiced only after a Master has opened the *Ananda Gandha chakra*. So there is no question of teaching the meditation to others.

Q. Can we practice the service anywhere or only in the healing service center?

Initially practice at the healing service center. Once you are tuned well, you can practice anywhere.

Q. *Every time you provide the service to a client, do you need to close your eyes?*

No. Only for the first few days you need to close your eyes and concentrate on the *Ananda Gandha* area while you do the healing prayer meditation. In a few days' time, you will become a master of the area! Even when you are walking, or simply sitting, you will see that the energy is continuously happening in you. So remember that the energy is happening and place your hand; that is enough. Nothing else is necessary; you need not necessarily close your eyes.

Q. *Swamiji, I am a doctor. I see many patients a day. How much time should I spend with each of them? You also said that our hands would drop automatically when the energizing is over.*

As far as you are concerned, you cannot afford to spend a lot of time with each patient. You just have to be in a meditative mood and treat them. Since you sit in your cabin continuously and treat the patients, the energy will be vibrating in that area. It is therefore enough if you simply spend time with them in the cabin. The energy will do the needful.

Q. *Should we do healing service in a separate area?*

No. You can do it in your own place, but try to do it in one place consistently.

Q. *Should we follow the same procedure for each client?*

Yes, follow the same procedure. Every time you remember my face, you will be just dragged into *Ananda Gandha chakra*. My face is like the gateway through which you can directly enter into *Ananda Gandha*. It is the key to enter *Ananda Gandha*.

Just remember my laughing face; you will just relax and enter the *chakra*. Afterwards, forgetting it will become a problem!

Q. Should we ask the clients to close their eyes?

It is better that you tell them to close their eyes. Otherwise, their eyes will wander and they will watch what you are doing! Tell them to close their eyes and remember the region where energy will be focused on during the service. For example, if you are focusing on *sahasrara chakra* during the healing meditation, tell them to remember their *sahasrara* region. Stop when the energy flow is complete.

Q. Is the energy that is going to others different from the energy within us?

Whether it flows into others or it flows within you, the energy is one and the same. Do not think that the energy has flowed away from you. Actually you are like a pipe through which energy flows. By flowing to others, it energizes you too. If you meditate without providing the service to others, the same energy is created within you and mixes with the surrounding air. Do not think that if you do not provide healing prayer service, the energy will be retained within yourself.

Q. Can we do Ananda Gandha meditation at all times?

Yes. It can be done anytime. It can be done all 24 hours also. If you are 24 hours in the *Ananda Gandha chakra*, you are actually in *Sahaja Samadhi*!

Q. What should we tell the client before healing?

Tell them about the seven *chakras* in the body. Tell them that diseases occur when the *chakras* are disturbed and that we can help the body heal when the *chakras* are energized.

We are directing positive energy flow to the *chakras* through meditation.

When the person himself meditates on the affected *chakra*, he can help his body heal. When another person meditates on that *chakra*, it is called healing prayer service. This is what we are doing.

They might question you as to how meditation and energy created by one reaches another. Albert Einstein clearly says that matter and energy are related. If I can give you matter in your hand, then I can surely give energy also in your hand. So both are the same; only the method is unknown to many. Since we know the method, we are able to do it.

Q. What should we think after we have finished the healing service?

At the end, just think, 'Let whatever is best happen.' Do not think that the person should get healed, etc. Do not pronounce any such affirmations. When you think that healing should happen, you are interfering with the *karma* of the person. Sometimes a potential cancer will be manifested as headache. If you heal the headache, it can come back as cancer. That is why you should think, 'Let whatever is good happen.' The energy will decide what to do. Energy is intelligence.

Q. Should we tell this statement aloud?

No. You just have to say it to yourself, not aloud.

Q. Can you repeat the meditation technique?

Close your eyes and concentrate on the area below *anahata* and above *manipuraka chakras*. Visualize the laughing face of the Master. The energy will begin to flow. Just relax into that energy. Do not generate, sustain or destroy any thoughts.

Brahma is the creator, Vishnu is the sustainer and Shiva is the destroyer. You will be *Parabrahman* (Supreme Self) if you do not generate, sustain, or destroy any thoughts, if you stay away from these three. Just be in the feeling, that's enough. Visualize that your being itself is laughter. The flowering in your body will exude from *Ananda Gandha chakra*.

Q. Can we lie down when meditating on the Ananda Gandha chakra?

Yes. You can meditate on *Ananda Gandha chakra* while you are in bed. You can meditate on it and drop into sleep. You can directly go to *samadhi* state when you deeply drop into *Ananda Gandha* in your sleep. Even when you wake up, the *Ananda Gandha chakra* will be active. Try to be in *Ananda Gandha* continuously.

Q. During the service, will the recipient feel the energy?

Yes. But do not worry about whether they have any such feeling. The result will be there, even if they do not feel anything.

Q. Will we feel the energy flow?

Yes. You will clearly feel the energy flow. Sometimes even if you do not feel it, the result will be there. That's what we ultimately want anyway.

Q. Why do I need to use the stick?

As a matter of social etiquette, when ladies do healing prayer service for men, and vice versa, please use the stick. It would be better if ladies stick to doing this service for ladies only, unless the male happens to be their relative.

Q. What happens if I lose the stick?

Do not lose it. If you lose it, contact the ashram directly. Do not make your own replacement.

Q. Can we completely cover the stick with metal covering?

Sure. You can enclose it in copper, silver or gold cases.

Q. Can our normal routine like work, etc be continued?

Yes. Your normal routine can continue. In fact, you will perform with more intelligence in your normal routine after being initiated.

Q. I have a doubt. This is off the track, but I wish to know - do masters curse people?

A master can never pronounce a curse. If he curses, he is not a master. There can be no anger where there is *gnana shakti* (true knowledge). Even if I curse, it can never come to pass!

Please understand that energy is compassion, energy is intelligence, energy is bliss.

Energy with compassion, intelligence and bliss forms four sides of the same pillar. One cannot exist without the other and if any one is missing, the person is not enlightened. When all four are present, it represents the super-conscious state. If any one is missing, it represents the unconscious state.

When *'atma shakti'* (energy of the soul) manifests itself through the head, it is intelligence. When it manifests itself through the *anahata chakra* or the heart, it is compassion. When it manifests itself through the being it is energy. When it does not manifest itself outside but remains inside, it is *ananda* or bliss. All four together are Enlightenment. So understand that a master can never curse. Only creativity can emanate from him, never destruction. The person who has realized the value of energy can only use it positively; only the one who has not realized the value of energy uses it negatively.

Q. Where should we store the stick?

Preferably in the *puja* room. It will be safe there!

Q. During healing service, should we play music and if so what music do we play?

Yes. The music will help both you and the person being healed to get into a meditative mood. You can play the Nithya *kirtans* during the healing service.

Q. What is the time duration that we have to follow for the healing service meditation?

For meditation on *Ananda Gandha*, spend 21 minutes. Healing meditation should be at least 3 to 5 minutes per *chakra*, per person. If you see 5 to 10 persons a day, you need not do the meditation separately.

Q. Should we wear white clothes?

Wear white clothes during the healing time. In other circumstances or times, do not worry about the white clothes.

Q. Can we do distance healing?

No. Distance healing cannot be done.

Q. How do we heal children? They might not close their eyes.

You can do a similar process for children also, even if their eyes are open.

Q. When do we do Shakthi Dharana?

Do *Shakti Dharana* before going to bed. After the *Shakti Dharana* meditation, in the bed, meditate on *Ananda Gandha* and drop off to sleep.

Q. Can little babies be healed?

Yes. Very small babies and children can also be healed.

Q. How do we heal contagious diseases?

Do not directly touch the infected area like in the case of a skin disease. Use the healing stick.

Q. Is there a special requirement for treating cancer?

Cancer is not infectious, so you can heal directly.

Q. Can we tell the patient that whatever is good for you will happen?

Yes, you can tell them.

Q. When will we be ready for healing?

Immediately after initiation. Quality control will be checked and approved!

Your Questions Answered

Q. Can women healers heal men without the healing stick?

No. Ladies should not heal men without the healing stick. Only if they are related, direct healing is fine. Doctors and professionals have no restrictions. In general, women should use healing sticks to heal men.

Q. Can we sit on the ground while healing?

Try your best to sit on some support while healing. Even the patient needs to be seated above the ground. Use chairs while healing. You should allocate a corner of your house or a room for healing. Even your *puja* room can be used for healing. Place Swamiji's picture, other articles and play the *kirtans* at least twice a day, morning and evening and start healing continuously.

Q. Can we direct critical cases to the ashram?

A. Sure.

Q. Can we heal touching the back part of the patient along with the front part corresponding to the **chakra***?*

A. Yes. You can heal touching the front and back part in the area of the relevant *chakra*.

Q: For how long can we do Ananda Gandha meditation?

You can be the whole day in *Ananda Gandha* meditation. Only in the beginning you need to close your eyes and meditate on the area. As you progress, you only have to think to drop into *Ananda Gandha*. You can drive your car and just stay in *Ananda Gandha*. You can be in it 24 hours a day.

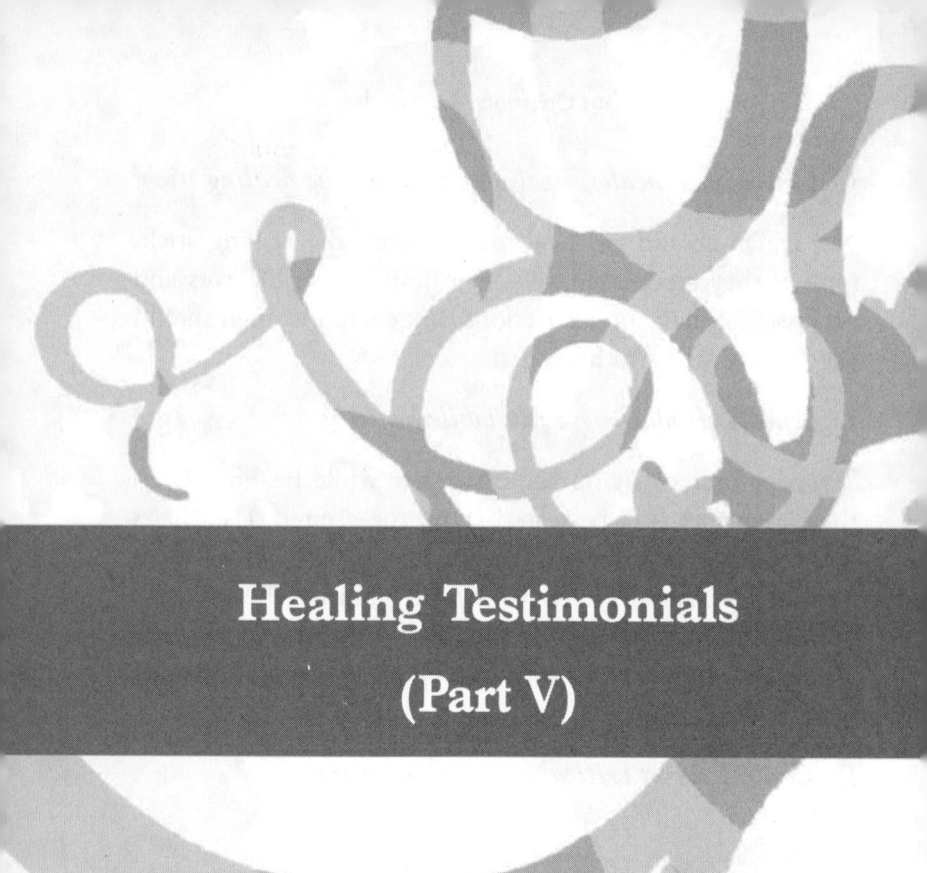

Healing Testimonials
(Part V)

Chapter 22
Healing Testimonials (Part V)

1. Dr. S.I. suffered from hereditary varicose veins. In winter and cold weather, his left foot used to swell up and it was very painful for him to move. Soon after initiation, I gave him 21 days of healing. At first the swelling subsided. Then the bluish tinge vanished and finally the pain stopped. Now, it only returns occasionally, especially when he has to work in extremely cold weather. Ten minutes of healing is all that is needed now. Remarkably, other family members have had to undergo surgery or other procedures for a temporary cure.

2. A five year old child, V.I. had severe seasonal allergies - eyes watering, nose blocking, and swelling of the face. It was caused by pollen in the air during spring and fall. The first healing brought the condition under control. As the child began to spend more time outside, giving the smallest dose of antihistamines and healing completely cured the child.

3. It was a time when I was proof-reading and preparing some newspaper articles. A big deadline was due for Jayanti, and I was proof-reading a book. The computer crashed and nothing would restart it again. All the data was locked in it. I gave healing to the laptop and switched it on again. This time it started. I copied the files and then it died out again. I later learnt that the motherboard had to be replaced and there were several

other issues with it. Without doubt it was the Master's grace that allowed me to continue with the work.

4. For four months, I gave healing to our car before I started it everyday. I had no idea why I did it, but it was a spontaneous action as if the car was asking for it. During this time, it went through the routine oil change and checking of the brakes and battery. One Friday morning, as I got ready to give it healing, I had a clear intuition - take it to the works today. At first the auto repair guys thought it was a joke. I insisted that they check it carefully, and sure enough all the brake pads were worn out, and the back wheels were no longer connected to the brakes! The work shop guys were astounded and shocked when I smiled. Little did they know that I was sending a deep prayer of thanks to Master!

5. A friend's son, 11 months old, poured scalding tea on his chest and got third degree burns. The friend requested for healing. Within three sessions, I found the child had healed considerably. After every session, he slept for 3 to 4 hours. When they took him to the doctor on the fourth day, she was astonished to see the degree of healing and said that the bandage was no longer required.

The father of this little boy had a torn ligament. His feet had swollen to an enormous size and he was in considerable pain. The first day of healing was a long session, lasting more than 30 minutes. The father slept deeply through the night. The next day, I was surprised to see him sitting and chatting with his friends. After 4 days of healing, he could walk again without crutches.

Healing Testimonials

He had not taken painkillers after the first day. His doctors were shocked to see him walk into the clinic on the fifth day without a crutch or heel support.

6. Dr. N.D. had trouble conceiving or carrying a baby full term. She had previously 6 miscarriages. Her current pregnancy was in the early first trimester when she called for help. She requested some help as doctors had told her that her baby had Down's syndrome. They advised her to abort the fetus. The heartbroken mother told this to a healer friend of mine and requested her help and support. She and I went to her for healing everyday. Every time I gave healing around *manipuraka chakra*, I could feel a butterfly-like fluttering. About 15 days later came her time to go to another town to test for Down's syndrome. She called us back on the way from the test and said she was worried that she would lose the baby. My friend and I rushed to her home to give her healing. As soon as I put my hand on her *manipuraka chakra* that day, I felt a surge of energy. Then all went blank and I was light.

   The mother carried the baby full term and delivered a healthy, happy baby. She named him Tage. Tage is now more than one year old.

7. The mother of a child who had chromosomal abnormality and suffered from repeated seizures requested healing. I told her right away that the mother shouldn't expect a cure or miracle. She understood and asked for support to stop seizures for the length of time possible. After 11 sessions, the child was having no seizures.

8. Prof. S. is one of the oldest Indian residents in Pullman. After having three heart attacks, and two bypass surgeries, the person has a pacemaker now. One day, he experienced pain in his chest and his friends took him to a hospital 2 hours away. The doctor said that the pacemaker had to be replaced and that his heart was not stable. He advised him to go back to California and be with his children. Then, a friend called me and requested healing for Prof. S. Two of us formed a relay team to give healing everyday, for 11 days. As the healing progressed, he began to feel a lot better. He reported that his breathing got better, and his chest didn't hurt as much. It was probably on the seventh day of healing when Master gave a beautiful experience. I was not aware of anything expect the tips of my fingers. They merged into the flesh and touched a beating heart. There, I felt something flipped inside, a tiny switch like thing. It was over in an instant, I have no clue as to what happened. But, Prof. S. slept deeply. At his next checkup, the doctors could find nothing wrong with his pacemaker!

9. Ms. P. had severe water retention, and couldn't sit or stand. She looked severely bloated. I gave her healing for about 15 minutes. When I finished, she was in a trance. Then, she suddenly jumped up and asked for the bathroom. Her friend said that it was wonderful to see her run to the bathroom!

Nithya Spiritual Healing
As a Service

Chapter 23

Nithya Spiritual Healing As a Service

The greatest service is to meditate for healing a person's pain. Anyone can provide food, clothing and material things. But can everyone help another heal? Now you are going to do that!

People ask me, 'How is it that so many healers are getting initiated?' Somehow, the reproducing formula has descended in this form. That is why hundreds and thousands of healers are getting reproduced through this form. One well-wisher of the ashram told me, *'Swamiji*, teach them meditation, but don't initiate them as spiritual healers. Let people come to you for healing service!' He said it with the hidden intention that the ashram should grow economically! I politely shook my head and came away.

You see, when I am gone, I don't want this healing science to be lost. When I leave this planet earth, I don't want this to leave with me. Let it become totally established.

For a long time, we have kept things a secret. What happened to the science of *siddha*? What happened to *Ayurveda*? Do you know that in Sushruta's time, they were doing open-heart surgeries? There are clear records to show that they have done brain surgeries and even plastic surgeries. Rambha and Menaka, the celestial beauties, might have had plastic surgery done on them!

Anyway, what happened to all that science? It got lost because of secrecy. I don't want to commit that mistake

Nithya Spiritual Healing as a Service

once more. If I keep it to myself, I will get name and fame, but the service to people will not happen. If I keep it to myself, things will get centralized and people will come from all over the world; money will pour in and we can have a big meditation hall! But real service to people will not happen.

If only I do the healing service, how many people can I handle? On the other hand, if all my healers also heal, how many millions of people can be helped! I want that for every 1000 people, there should be one Nithya spiritual healer! In every city, there should be at least 1000 healers.

People ask me, 'But what will happen to the doctor's profession?'

Please rest assured: the doctor's profession will not get disturbed. There are thousands and thousands of doctors getting created. Is the number of patients reducing? No!

One more thing - with supplementary systems of spiritual healing coming up, doctors can spend their time on research work. Don't think that doctors are only for curing diseases. There are so many positive things that they can do. They can focus on research to elongate life, create new systems, create new medicines etc.

Understand, Nithya Spiritual Healers' Initiation is the ultimate technique that you can receive from the Master.

Be very clear: When you have conducted spiritual healing services for 1000 people, you have actually taken 1000 steps towards your own enlightenment. We operate on the principle that when you change the frequency inside you through prayer and meditation, the frequency in the outer world also changes.

When the mind changes, matter changes. This is the truth. This is the principle by which, when you go inside yourself, you automatically radiate energy around you.

THE SAME POWER OF HEALING OF THE MASTER IS WITH THE HEALER

One man asked me, '*Swamiji*, you say that you have initiated us in *Ananda Gandha chakra* to heal like how you heal. Then why are we not able to heal like you heal?' Be very clear: if I have a six inch pipe in me to heal, I have given the same diameter pipe to you also. Don't think that I have given a smaller diameter pipe to you. The problem is, you have blocked your pipe with these kinds of mental blockages. If you understand these points I have told you and remove these blockages, even more energy than what flows in my body will flow in you. The important thing is, you should take up responsibility.

MODES OF SERVICE

There are various means by which you can spread the message of bliss and health through Nithya Spiritual Healing.

FREE NITHYA SPIRITUAL HEALING CENTERS

The basic thing that can and should be done by every initiated healer is to run a Nithya Spiritual Healing Center at your place. You can keep a separate room for providing healing service. Every day, allot a time for the healing service. Make this time known to people so they know about the availability of the service. You can put up the title board that we provide so that people will know the location of the healing center. You could put a board or banner etc. to publicize the timings of the healing provided everyday. This is a beautiful way to not only provide service but to keep the bliss flowing inside you continuously and to keep your connection with me alive.

FREE NITHYA SPIRITUAL HEALING CAMPS

You can organize free Nithya Spiritual Healing Camps in your locality regularly. This can help reach out to many more people than through the healing center only. The free healing camps can be organized in the areas of economically weaker sections of society, so that we can cater to their basic healthcare needs and they can avail themselves of the healing service.

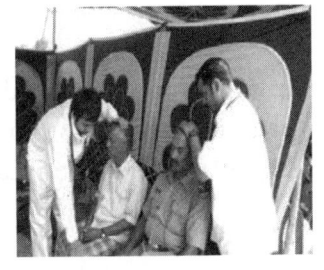

Healing camp in Vancouver, Canada

Healing camp in Bangalore

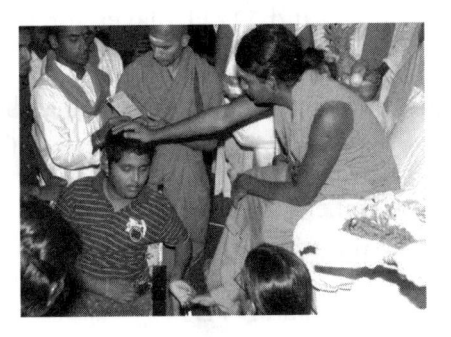

Swamiji healing at Bidadi ashram

Dhyanapeetam Healing Temples

Dhyanapeetam Healing Temples are energy fields – the source of collective positive energy.

Each Healing Temple should have its own:

- Spiritual Head (SH)
- Administrative Head (AH)
- Accountant
- Galleria in-charge

The training for people to hold the above positions is provided at the headquarters of Nithyananda Mission in Bidadi, India.

All the infrastructure needed to conduct *satsangs* (spiritual gathering), provide healing and spread the message of Master should be available at the Healing Temple.

The facilities needed include:

- Meditation hall
- Electronic equipment like
    - TV and DVD player for playing video discourses
    - Audio system for playing audio discourses and *kirtans* (music in praise of the Divine)
- Life Bliss Galleria items
    - Books
    - CDs and DVDs

- Energized products – *rudraksha mala* (necklace strung with *rudraksh* beads), red sandalwood *mala*, bracelet, *kumkum* (vermilion), *yantras* (a diagramaatic 2-D representation of the cosmos on a copper plate), etc...
- Information and subscription for magazines
  - Nithyanandam (3 months)
  - Nithya Dhyaan (weekly)
- Reception and office requirements
  - Application for free healing
  - Participant card for free healing service
  - Reminiscences form to note down the experiences of people before and after healing
  - Pamphlets on the various program offerings of Nithyananda Mission

All of the above can be obtained from the Bidadi ashram.

The recommended routine at Dhyanapeetam Healing Temples is from 6:15 pm to 9:15 pm every day.

6:15 pm – Nithya Dhyaan meditation

7:00 pm – *Aarti* (Offering lit camphor)

7:30 pm – Healing (with mild music *kirtans*)

On Sundays, healing will be followed by half an hour of *kirtans / bhajans*.

Healing Testimonials (Part VI)

Chapter 24
Healing Testimonials (Part VI)

1. I am a professional who had to quit my job because of a chronic heel pain; it was such a pulling pain that I had for over 6 years. It became so bad that I could not walk. I used to walk without my left heel touching the ground, literally hopping, and this was just when I was in my forties. I tried various systems of medicine and alternative healing but they were just temporary respites if at all any. As destiny would have it, I attended LBP Level 2 - NSP with Swamiji. At the end of NSP, during Energy Darshan, when I went up to Swamiji and told Him about my problem, He smiled and said, 'I will take care.' Little did I realize then that these were not mere words, it was a promise. He really took care. When I stepped out of the hall after *darshan,* I had no pain and the pain never came back. It has been more than 3 years now. I have got a job now. I do my meditation regularly. I have so much more energy and am able to walk long distances. Whenever I keep my feet down, I am filled with gratitude to Swamiji.

   Chandra Murthy, Mumbai

2. I had been diagnosed with Polycystic Ovarian Syndrome (PCOS), which can and had caused severe hormonal issues. It was detected through an ultrasound which showed that my ovaries were just covered in cysts and in huge masses, so much so that there was no distinguishing between cysts. I was under hormone

treatment and it was under control but there could be complications in the future.

In May 2006, Swamiji did Dhyana Spurana Program (DSP) in Oklahoma City. That was my first meditation program and the beginning of a new life for me. After DSP, I felt like a huge cloud that I didn't even know existed, had lifted. The peace, vibrancy and intensity that I felt after that could not even be described and a deep sense of fulfillment settled over me.

One day while leaving the hall, Swamiji happened to walk by and He stopped and looked at me and said, 'Ma, some problem is there with...(and He looked up for a while), some disturbance is there in *muladhara*'. I looked at Him with utter disbelief, because it is not common knowledge and I was dumbfounded and just nodded, wondering how He could have known. Then He looked at me intensely and waved His hand and said, 'You will be healed!' and continued walking.

About a month after the program, I realized I had lost 30 pounds, which I had battled with for a long time, having been close to 200 pounds and not able to lose the weight even through diet and exercise. That is how I realized how emotionally related my weight had been. During one of Swamiji's discourses, He had mentioned how any addiction is a call for fulfillment. He said you will look externally for fulfillment but you will only be filled and not fulfilled. I had never confronted the fact that my obesity was just the want to fill a void, to fill an 'emptiness'.

It took a whole year before I went in for an ultrasound. After being there for an hour, the radiologist looked at me and asked me why I had come in for an ultrasound (because a physician won't generally refer you for one unless you are pregnant). I told her it was because I had severe PCOS and she looked really confused. She showed me where my ovaries were and I just could not believe how there were small shadows. The radiologist said that it looked like there used to be some cysts or masses but there was nothing there anymore.

I also used to have problems with allergies. My face used to swell and my eyes used to water. It was pretty hard to function with such symptoms. Now I have none of that and even though seasonal allergies is a huge problem in Oklahoma, I am unaffected by it anymore. This really made me believe in all of those health issues being psychosomatic.

Ma Nithyananda Sevika

3. I had diabetes for ten years. My sugar count used to go as high as 440. Then I started having slight heart pain also. I came to Swamiji for healing during the one month of free healing service he was giving in March 2008. After the healing, my diabetes came totally under control. My heart complaint is also gone. I feel much more peaceful and am organizing group meditations in our house also.

D. Sivashanmugam, 49 years, Tamil Nadu

4. On February 9 2008, I fell down and had a fracture in my left leg. The doctor said I needed surgery and

implantation. I had severe pain and was not able to walk at all due to unbearable pain. I was crying profusely when I came to Swamiji for healing in March 2008 during the month-long free healing camp. By the third day of healing itself, the pain reduced considerably, and I was able to walk by myself with just a little support. I even climbed the stairs myself to go to Swamiji for healing!

L. Shakti, Bangalore

5. I had a problem of passing too much protein in my urine. There was severe pain and swelling in both my legs. I came for the free healing camp to Swamiji and am now completely healed. There is no swelling or pain in the legs. Even the doctor is amazed at the improvement.

K. Palanisami, 54 years, Tamil Nadu

6. I have been having migraine for 6 years and wheezing problem since one year. I did all the investigations like scan, X-ray etc. and tried various systems of medicine like allopathy, ayurveda and homeopathy but I got no relief. I came to Swamiji for the healing camp and on the first day itself, my headache disappeared and has not come back since.

Vasanthi, 33 years, Bangalore

Healers' Meet - August 9, 2006

Chapter 25
Healers' Meet - August 9, 2006

(The following is the message of Paramahamsa Nithyananda on the Healers' Meet, - August 9, 2006.)

I welcome you all with my love and respect.

WHY HEALERS' MEET

First, let me share with you why we have this healers' meet. I want to keep one whole day for meditation for the healers. Otherwise, you have so many distractions at home. This healers' meet is so that you get a full day to spend in the energy field. This is a means for you to rejuvenate yourself. This is the opportunity to spend a full day living in *Ananda Gandha*.

WHY *ANANDA GANDHA* MEDITATION

When you do *Ananda Gandha* meditation every day, continuously, nothing from the outside can shake you inside. Even if everything around you is falling, you will be stable and strong.

It gives you:

1. *Sat*: Clarity in everything

    We will not get cheated. Why do we get cheated? Because we are all driven by greed for something or fear of something. It is very easy for anyone to cheat us. Don't think we are all very intelligent and that it is difficult to cheat us!

All the person needs to do is build a fantasy that matches our greed. To prove we are intelligent, we will check four or five points and if they are fine, we will simply do what he says.

A director can in 10 minutes build a fantasy world to entice a producer to fund the production. The director shows that a film has become a big hit, there is money pouring in, the producer is becoming a millionaire, there is a line of actors and actresses waiting to sign the next film with him, etc. By the time the producer hears all this, he has already lived this fantasy...and signed the check.

When you do *Ananda Gandha* meditation, you will have clarity because you can see things objectively without being driven by greed and fear.

2. *Chit*: Consciousness

   You will have enthusiasm for everything you do. The very skin, the cells, will radiate energy and enthusiasm. You will simply take and execute decisions one after another without feeling tired, and more importantly, with the same enthusiasm and intelligence.

3. *Ananda*: Bliss for no reason

   All of us have got doctorates in how to be sad for no reason! With *Ananda Gandha* meditation, you will learn how to be happy for no reason.

THREE CATEGORIES OF HEALERS

All healers fall within three categories:

You see, I have given all of you initiation into *Ananda Gandha* which is like giving you a diamond.

However, all of you are not able to recognize this gift or use this as a diamond.

The first category of healers treats the diamond like a vegetable-cutter. These are the people who have taken initiation only to use the healers' badge to enter the Ananda Sabha (meditation hall) for our various programs, enjoy the program and leave. The gift of *Ananda Gandha* is used as a means of entertainment!

The second category of healers is those who use *Ananda Gandha* just as a paper-weight is used by a cloth merchant. They are not committed to the initiation or the service. They just use it to heal a few people once in a while.

The third category of healers is those who use *Ananda Gandha* initiation like how a jeweler would use a diamond. They put the diamond to the use it is meant for. They are the ones who practice the meditation every single moment and use the meditation to gain inner strength. They are constantly connected to me.

MEDITATIONS TO BE DONE BY ALL HEALERS

1. Do *Ananda Gandha* meditation immediately after getting up in the morning. Just sit in your bed for 5 minutes and do the meditation. Just like there is a truth behind astrology and why the planet and star positions at the time of birth affect your whole life (though astrology is totally misunderstood and misused now), similarly, how you get up in the morning affects your whole day.

2. Whenever you have time, say when you get a break in office, just after reaching the office etc, do *Ananda Gandha* meditation. You just have to spend 2-3 minutes, and you can see how the task you do next, happens beautifully.

3. Do your meditations everyday. Do *Ananda Gandha* meditation for at least 21 minutes every morning. Do *Shakti Dharana* meditation every night. Do *Nithya Dhyaan* meditation every day.

Healing Products

Chapter 26
Healing Products
(Special Feature)

Nithya Spiritual Healers can use and provide various healing products to help themselves, and the persons being healed.

Rudraksha Mala

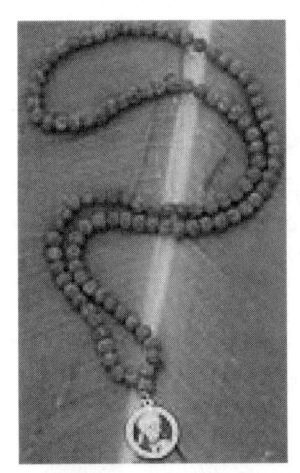

Rudraksha mala is the chain of energized *rudraksha* beads energized personally by Paramahamsa Nithyananda. *Rudraksha* has the capacity to store cosmic energy in it, just like how a battery stores electricity. The energy generated during the daily Nithya Dhyaan meditation is stored in the *rudraksha mala* and is available for use throughout the day.

Figure 14: Rudraksha Mala

We should know an important law of Existence: the thoughts that we think and the feelings that we radiate affect not only us but also our surroundings, the nation, the whole world and the universe. When we radiate negative or low feelings from inside us, we are very much contributing to the collective negativity. Similarly, when we are blissful inside ourselves, we are directly adding to the positive collective consciousness and thus we attract fortune. The energized *rudraksha mala* is a storehouse of the positive cosmic energy.

Actually, we have three kinds of spaces. The *chittakasha* is the inner space within us. The *ghataakasha* is the space that surrounds us. Since emotions and thoughts affect the space around us, the *chittakasha* affects the *ghataakasha* and vice versa. The *rudraksha* radiates positive energy into the *ghataakasha* which naturally radiates it back and benefits the *chittakasha*, the inner space of the individual.

Rudraksha, with its energy properties, has benefits of its own. Similarly, meditation has benefits for the meditator. These two can be combined to have benefits many times over if the person wearing the *rudraksha* is a meditator.

Being an energy source, the *rudraksha* has powerful healing properties. It has the power to restore physical health and mental wellbeing by putting one in touch with the source of energy inside each of us. If you are not well, you can hold on to the *rudraksha mala* and meditate for a few minutes, connecting with the pure cosmic energy. The body has natural intelligence and self-healing properties. The *rudraksha* reinforces the natural healing power of the body to overcome the disease and restore health.

RED SANDALWOOD *MALA*

The red sandalwood *mala* is a chain of beads of red sandalwood. It is energized personally by Paramahamsa. Just like *rudraksha*, it has the power to store energy in it like a battery. The mala can be worn throughout the day. It will hold the energy of meditation in it.

Figure 15: Red Sandalwood Mala

Healing Products

NITHYANANDAM BRACELET

Figure 16: Nithyanandam Bracelet

The Nithyanandam bracelet is a constant reminder to live every moment in meditation.

'*Nithyanandam*' written on the bracelet reminds one of the state we are all actually in and are striving to be consciously aware of - *nithya ananda* or eternal bliss. The bracelet, energized by Paramahamsa also serves as a protection bracelet when worn throughout the day.

KUMKUM (VERMILION MARK)

The *kumkum* is the red powder that is applied on the forehead between the eyebrows at the location of the *ajna chakra*. By its very property, it energizes the *ajna chakra*. Also, because you have the *kumkum* on the *ajna*, constantly you have the awareness of *ajna chakra*.

Figure 17: Kumkum and Paste

Ajna chakra is the master *chakra* and the characteristic of this *chakra* is that to energize it, just being aware of it is powerful enough. The *kumkum* thus directly aids in energizing the *ajna chakra*. The *kumkum* from Nithyananda Dhyanapeetam is also energized by Paramahamsa himself. So, the benefits are even greater.

Vibhuti

Vibhuti is the holy ash that is usually smeared on the forehead. Metaphysically, the significance of *vibhuti* is to remind one constantly about the ephemeral nature of life, that we are going to be reduced to ashes one day. The energized *vibhuti* is a powerful energy medicine. Whether it is skin disease or common cold or physical pains, etc., you can apply the *vibhuti* on the affected part along with healing. You can also put a pinch of *vibhuti* in water and drink the water. There are countless testimonials from around the world of the *vibhuti* doing miracles, whether in the physical, mental or spiritual plane. *Vibhuti* is available at Nithyananda *vedic* temples.

Figure 18: Sri Chakra Yantras

Yantras

Yantras are meditation aids energized by Paramahamsa. For example, the *Sri Chakra yantra* is actually a powerful mystical 2D representation of the cosmos (*brahmaanda*) and a representation of our own body (*pindaanda*). It has 43 triangles in nine concentric circles, each representing deeper layers of ourselves.

Inside our body we have 43 energies: the energy to breathe, express anger, lust, the energy to see, etc. All these functions

Healing Products

are brought about by these 43 energies in our system. If we integrate all 43 energies towards one point, we are enlightened. By continually visualizing the diagram of the *yantra* we have the experience of it – enlightenment.

Sitting on the *yantra* while meditating aids the meditation and enhances the energy flow in the meditator. You can also keep it in the *puja* room as an item of worship. The *Sri Chakra Yantra* is worshipped during the very powerful meditation, *Sri Vidya puja*.

To know more about the energized products, please visit www.lifeblissgalleria.com

Healers' Meet - December 30, 2006

Chapter 27
Healers' Meet - December 30, 2006

(The following is the message of Paramahamsa Nithyananda on the occasion of *Brahmotsavam* - Healers' Day, December 30, 2006.)

Shankara says beautifully, 'Three things are difficult in life. First is *manushyatva*, the human birth. The second, which is rarer is *mumukshatva*, having the desire and urge to search for a consciousness beyond ordinary human life. The third and the rarest is *mahapurusha-sangam*, being with an enlightened master and having his *darshan*.'

Of 10 million living beings, only 1000 get human birth. Of the 1000 human beings, hardly 10 strive for knowing the Truth and of those 10, hardly 1 or 2 meet a master.

Whether you realize it or not, all you healers assembled here have got all these three. You have a human body. You have the urge to know the Truth. If it had not been so, you would not have sat for our Life Bliss meditation programs - ASP, NSP, BSP and then the Healers' Initiation. And you have a living, enlightened master with you. If you have these three and still miss the goal, your life is wasted.

Sat Chit Ananda, all three will exist together if you are in the ultimate consciousness. They are all one consciousness. *Sat* (truth), *Chit* (consciousness) and *Ananda* (bliss) will exist together in the ultimate state.

Being in *Ananda Gandha* will not only give good physical and mental health but will also give you the clarity to handle anything that happens in the outer world.

You will be able to handle your emotions properly. Take anger for example. As of now, if you are angry with someone, after shouting at the other person, the fire will burn you as much as it burnt him. You will be disturbed for the same half hour that the other person is disturbed.

But, if you are in *Ananda Gandha*, you will have the clarity and awareness to use the anger but be completely unaffected by it.

It is like using a knife to cut vegetables. You pick up the knife to cut vegetables and when you have finished cutting, you put it down. Do you always carry the knife with you saying that your job is to cut vegetables?

Healing is just a side-effect of *Ananda Gandha* meditation. The real effect is the transformation that happens in you and your consciousness. It is not even just growth, it is a quantum leap to a different plane.

Stay in *Ananda Gandha* 24 hours a day, whether you are eating, driving or breathing. The gateway to *Ananda Gandha* is in the region above *manipuraka chakra* and below *anahata chakra*. Understand, this is the gateway to *Ananda Gandha* in the physical body; *Ananda Gandha* actually exists beyond the physical body.

Initially, you might be doing *Ananda Gandha* meditation for half an hour every day. The mind will wander and you will try to bring awareness to *Ananda Gandha* whenever you remember. Ultimately, you should be in *Ananda Gandha* 24 hours a day.

I am not saying you should force yourself and concentrate on *Ananda Gandha chakra*. Just bring your awareness to *Ananda Gandha* constantly, in a relaxed mood.

Be in *Ananda Gandha* for the next 24 hours. When you are really in *Ananda Gandha*, you are beyond body consciousness. If you are truly in *Ananda Gandha*, in the evening, when we have the fire-walking, you will not feel you are walking on fire. You will feel you are walking on a bed of flowers rather than a bed of fire!

Healing Testimonials
(Part VII)

Chapter 28
Healing Testimonials (Part VII)

1. I have been suffering from pain in my back in various places, extending to pain in my legs. I used to feel heaviness in different parts of my body. After Nithya Spiritual Healing, my body feels light like cotton. The back pain has vanished. I feel I have got out fresh from deep sleep.

   S. Radha, 54 years, Chennai

2. For the past 8-10 years, I have been having a lot of skin problems. Some doctors diagnosed it as fungal infection, some said it was eczema and some said it was psoriasis. In spite of all the treatment, the condition did not improve. Instead, the whole body got affected.

   Before I came to the healing camp, the skin on my whole body was affected. There was pus, blood and some kind of fluid oozing from the neck region. When Swamiji touched the neck region (in spite of all the above symptoms, He placed his hand on the affected region - what compassion!), the very next day it dried up! After three to four days, even the itching stopped. Now my skin is completely healed.

   Suraj R., 38 years, Karnataka

3. I suffered from a chronic lack of sleep, due to the seemingly permanent shift in my body clock by more than four to five hours. It meant that anywhere in the

world I traveled, I used to always sleep only by 2 am or 3 am. Having to get up early in the morning left me disoriented and extremely tired throughout the day. I was accumulating stress for the past 15 years.

I was extremely fortunate to be healed by Swamiji on 10th March, 2008. Swamiji advised me to stop all medications like the melatonin which I was taking and blessed me saying I was healed.

The first few days since 10th March left me extremely sleepy during the whole day. Then, I was amazed at the changes in my sleep patterns. Since then I have started to go to bed between 10 pm and 11 pm, and have promptly gone off to sleep. All the sleep troubles I experienced for the past 15 years seem to have gone away in the past two weeks. I no longer dread going to bed every night, and staying awake all night. My heartfelt thanks to Swamiji for His grace!

Raajesh Iyer, 37 years, Bangalore

4. I had both sides of my fallopian tubes blocked. The doctor, after seeing the laparoscopy report, said that no treatment would help and there was no chance for me to bear a child. I was advised to go in for a test-tube baby.

Swamiji healed me in March 2005 and my fallopian tubes got completely healed. In April 2005, I was pregnant. My girl was born on 1 November, 2005.

K. Nagammai, Tamil Nadu

5. I used to have great difficulty in drinking and swallowing. There was lot of body pain, and a migraine-like pain in the head.

After five days of healing from Swamiji, I am happy to humbly report the changes in my health and mind. My cervical spondilitis has considerably improved. My esophagus structure also is improving and I feel full of strength. I am able to travel from Sunkadkatte to Dhyanapeetam everyday by bus till date. This is proof enough of Swamiji's healing which is working on me.

Nigar Sultana, 58 years, Bangalore

6. I was admitted to Apollo Hospital on 25th December, 2007 following high fever and fits. Soon, I slipped into coma. The doctors first treated me for brain fever but after the diagnosis, they said that 50% of my brain was infected and affected. While I was in hospital, my folks were not satisfied with my recovery as the doctors could not proceed in any direction. Since my uncle is a Nithyananda devotee and has faith in the Nithya Spiritual Healing technique, he contacted a healer in Chennai and my healing was started immediately in the ICU of the hospital. After three days of healing itself, my condition showed a lot of improvement. Even though the doctors were not done with their diagnosis, the medicines started working on my body. After 20 days of healing, I was discharged from the hospital in good condition.

P. Nandakumar, 25 years, Chennai

7. I was diagnosed with leukemia in October 2004. I soon learned that it was one of the greatest gifts of my life because it brought me to my *sadguru*, Swamiji. Soon after starting treatment, a neighbor called and said her niece, who lived five hours from me, was a Nithya Spiritual Healer who felt drawn to offer me healing when she heard of my diagnosis. That in itself was a healing since I was stunned that someone I didn't even know was willing to drive so far to assist me. The healer wouldn't even take a dime from me to cover her travel expenses and only suggested that I take the Life Bliss Program Level 1 to extend the healing and later have the chance to meet Swamiji. I was fortunate enough to do both and more!

During the healing session, I felt relaxed and noticed lightness and a feeling that I had no boundary, especially around my head area. The symptoms and side effects from the drugs immediately subsided and my appetite improved. At the end of March 2005 my life took a dramatic turn when I attended the NSP with Swamiji in Seattle. Three weeks later I had a bone marrow biopsy. The oncologist was so surprised by the results that he called me on the weekend to say that my body was in complete cellular remission! It was a gift from Existence/Swamiji that I had gone into such a complete remission on such a small dose of medicine in such a short timeframe. I enjoy robust energy and vibrant health now, especially with the Nithya Dhyan meditation and Nithya Yoga.

Ma Nithyananda Prajna, Washington, USA

Living in
Ananda Gandha

Chapter 29

Living in *Ananda Gandha*

(*'Living in Ananda Gandha' is a one-day program that shows the various techniques to live every moment in Ananda Gandha. The following is an extract from the program)

LIVING IN *ANANDA GANDHA* IS ENLIGHTENMENT

Living in *Ananda Gandha* is enlightenment. Whenever you live in *Ananda Gandha*, you are enlightened. In all those moments of being in *Ananda Gandha*, you are enlightened. In those minutes, whether you are aware of it or not, you are living your enlightenment even though, in that moment, your consciousness is not expanded enough to imbibe or understand all the changes happening inside your system during *Ananda Gandha* meditation or during healing.

ANANDA GANDHA - CONNECTION TO COSMIC INTELLIGENCE

And in one more dimension, this *Anandha Gandha* initiation is not just activating your automatic intelligence, it is connecting with cosmic intelligence. The very opening of *Ananda Gandha* is an activation of your automatic intelligence. The same opening is acting as a connection to cosmic intelligence which runs the whole show.

Through *Ananda Gandha* initiation, your *Ananda Gandha* is connected with the cosmic *Ananda Gandha*. You become a part of the Whole when you heal.

You are the Center of the Universe

In the Vignana Bhairava Tantra, the encyclopedia of techniques for enlightenment, Shiva says, 'You are the center of the universe.' This statement is applicable to all the billions of people who are present in the world now. This statement is not just applicable to only a single person. 'You are the center of the universe' is applicable to everyone. That means six billion centers of the universe exist. But how can that be? Center means one. Only then it can be called the 'center'. Otherwise the very definition doesn't fit. We can make this point. But, Shiva clearly declares, 'You are the center of the universe.'

By the word 'center' He means *Ananda Gandha*. *Ananda Gandha* is in a different plane; it is in a totally different plane. When you live in the body, when your awareness is in the body, if you see the master, you will note the six feet or 10 feet distance between you and him. When you go deep into *Ananda Gandha*, you will experience that no difference exists between him and you.

Can you think that your hand holding this book is something different from your body? But if a doll is kept here near you, you think the doll is separate from you. You don't feel any discontinuity with your hand. You are able to relate with your physical body because you are in the physical body. You are not able to relate with the other things because you have not reached the etheric body and deeper energy bodies. If you touch the etheric body, you will feel all things are one and the same. In just the way that you feel that the lower arm and hand are the extension of the body, you will feel that the mic and the chair and everything around you is an extension of your being.

And if you go deep into your being, if you go deep into *Ananda Gandha,* just as you feel the blissful feeling in *Ananda Gandha,* you will sense that even in each and every stone the energy of the cosmos exists. You will see the same bubbling energy, the same bubbling blissfulness happening inside your system, in each and every atom of whatever you see. Just as you feel alive inside your skin, you will feel the same aliveness in the chair, the table, the sofa, the flower, in everything.

When you realize this, you become that energy. Until you realize it, you are something different from that energy. Once you realize it, you become that energy. And you becoming that energy is what Shiva means by, 'You are the center of the universe.'

When you are in that state, you feel you are the center of the universe because you can feel yourself in everything.

Our *Ananda Gandha* is an Extension of master's *Ananda Gandha*

Ananda Gandha deeksha (initiation) is the connection to cosmic energy, the master's energy. Our *Ananda Gandha* is an extension of his *Ananda Gandha.* Just as your little finger is an extension of your own body, each person's *Ananda Gandha* is the extension of the Master's *Ananda Gandha.* That is why whenever we offer healing, people are able to feel the same energy as the Master's. If he touches someone, his or her headache or cancer gets healed; if we touch, the same thing happens. Because of his presence, all the miracles happen through us also.

Research findings...

In an experiment with cells, a cell was taken from a body. From that cell the DNA, the basic building block of life, was isolated. DNA is considered responsible for our hormones, behavior and much more. The DNA segment was removed and kept in a medium. It no longer had any connection with the body directly. There was no physical connection between the DNA and the body.

Next, the subject was stimulated to express an emotion. The result was shocking - the very hormones released in the person's body were also released at that particular time by the DNA which was outside the body. This was repeated multiple times in various places and the same result was observed. Whether anger or fantasy or fear, the same hormones released inside the the subject's body were secreted in the subject's DNA, kept in another medium.

The master's DNA is enough to put you in bliss, to put you in enlightenment and to enable you to radiate his quality, to radiate his nature and become him because the *Ananda Gandha* inside every one of us is the DNA of God. As Paramahamsa states, 'I am not here to prove that I am divine. I am here to prove that *you* are divine!'

DNA Phantom Effect

(Based on research done by a world-renowned quantum physicist, Dr. Poponin, Institute of Heart Math)

In this experiment, the characteristics of light - photons were studied in a light scattering chamber. The graph looked like a typical plot representing random motion of the photons (background random noise counts of the photomultiplier).

> Next, a DNA sample was placed in the scattering chamber. The graph now changed showing an interaction between the DNA and the photons of light.
>
> Then the DNA was removed from the chamber. When the DNA is removed, one anticipates that the graph will be the same as before the DNA was placed in the chamber. Surprisingly, the graph after the removal of the DNA from the scattering chamber looked distinctly different from the one obtained before the DNA was placed in the chamber.
>
> In spite of the removal of the DNA, it influenced the behavior of the light - photons. Not only immediately upon removal but for several more days, the lingering effect of the DNA on the light-photons persisted.
>
> So, one can conclude that the consciousness from a particular object or a particular person is always radiating and it contributes its own effect. We can also note that in nature, the higher forms of consciousness, by their very presence, will influence the other forms of lower consciousness.
>
> The complete paper is available at:
> http://twm.co.nz/DNAPhantom.htm

Master radiates a higher consciousness than ordinary human beings. His presence directly influences everyone around him. The initiated healers, when in *Ananda Gandha*, are in the same high consciousness as the master. So naturally they will also be influencing the very atmosphere around them.

If we radiate and spread *Ananda Gandha* energy in the world, we will be blissful. Secondly, we will automatically positively influence the people and environment around us.

Cloning Enlightenment

From a cell, you can create another cell using the nucleus for replication. In the same way, from a body, another God can be created by a *deeksha*. That is the whole principle and science behind *cloning enlightenment*.

The healers are the bodies for enlightenment cloning. If you are ready to surrender your ego, the only requirement, you will find that you are transformed.

Inside every one of us is the potential to blossom into enlightened consciousness, just as each bud contains the potential to flower. We have Godliness as our core, waiting to flower into bliss. The quality of the flower in each bud is sitting quietly within it. In the same way, the expanded God consciousness is within each and every one of us waiting to flower.

Living 24 Hours in *Ananda Gandha*

Right now we are generally operating and doing everything from the brain, from the head. Whether it is seeing, hearing, feeling or decision-making, the instructions are coming from our heads. We are controlling the whole body from the head, without any conscious effort.

Now decide that whatever you do, you will execute all activities from *Ananda Gandha*. All of you initiated healers have a direct conscious experience with me. So even just a photograph, a *kirtan* or a thought of me will pull you towards *Ananda Gandha*. That is the means to enter *Ananda Gandha* at any time.

Don't do anything from the head. Do everything from *Ananda Gandha* – what you know as *Ananda Gandha*. As of now you think the nose is inhaling. Inhale instead from *Ananda Gandha*. Now the lung is exhaling. Exhale from *Ananda Gandha*.

Now the brain is thinking. Instead think from *Ananda Gandha*. Sense from *Ananda Gandha*. Move the body from *Ananda Gandha*. As of now, you are taking food for the stomach through the throat. Put the food through *Ananda Gandha*. Let the whole center be shifted and concentrated towards *Ananda Gandha*.

You currently think you hear a song through your ears. Now, hear the song from *Ananda Gandha*. Let the song directly fall on *Ananda Gandha*, not on the ear. Let the sound descend on *Ananda Gandha*.

Smell in *Ananda Gandha*. Think in *Ananda Gandha*. Inhale from *Ananda Gandha*. Exhale from *Ananda Gandha*. Even as you walk, move the body from *Ananda Gandha*. Do everything from *Ananda Gandha*. Whatever is listed and all that is not listed - do everything from *Ananda Gandha*.

All this activity will simply push you towards *Ananda Gandha*. Once you go to the entrance, there is no need for further movement. It will pull you from there, because that is the *ananda* sucking force. It will swallow all of your peripheral centers. And it will become one center.

ANNAMAYA KOSHA MEDITATION TECHNIQUE

This meditation is intended to guide you to live in *Ananda Gandha* in the physical level.

From *Ananda Gandha* involve all the activities of the five senses. As of now, if you open your eyes, you will see something.

Living in Ananda Gandha

Whatever is in front of you, you will see. But we have never seen things as they are. Once your inner eye is awakened, you will see things as they are; you will see reality as it is. As of now, whatever we are seeing as reality is just one more dream. As long as the mind is there, whatever we see in the world is still partial; it is not whole. Now, from *Ananda Gandha*, focus your awareness on your eyes.

Please be clear: this is not attention. This is not concentration. If you do this, you are again using the mind. Concentration, attention, all those things are more thought – one more pressure. Just relax and allow the awareness to travel towards the eyes. Let the eyes fill with bliss energy. With this awareness, slowly open your eyelids and look at the area where you are sitting. It is a trial to involve the vision from *Ananda Gandha*.

See the things in the hall. See the activities going on around you from *Ananda Gandha*, not just from the eyes. Don't see things through your eyeballs but from your *Ananda Gandha*. Let your vision come from *Ananda Gandha*. If you involve your vision in *Ananda Gandha*, you will see a new glow, a new light. You will see a different ambience in the same area where you are sitting.

Slowly close your eyelids. Now involve the auditory sense in *Ananda Gandha*. From *Ananda Gandha*, allow the bliss energy to spread and occupy the hearing apparatus. Start hearing from *Ananda Gandha* whatever sounds there are in the room. Let *Ananda Gandha* hear all the subtle sounds. So many thousands of sound waves are reaching you.

Now involve both eyes and ears. See and hear from *Ananda Gandha*.

Next, we are going to involve taste. Involve the whole mouth in bliss energy. From *Ananda Gandha*, allow the bliss energy to involve the taste sense. Let the tongue become as sensitive and relaxed as possible. Let everything that exists in your oral cavity become sensitive. Be aware of the whole oral cavity – the teeth, the tongue, the tonsils, the mouth and the throat. With this sensitivity, put the sweet in your mouth. Take the sweet and allow it to dissolve. Don't try to eat it. Don't try to move your tongue. Open your mouth and put the sweet inside. The instinct will come and you will try to move the tongue. Don't do anything. Just be aware. Enjoy the different feeling. Experience a different awareness exploding there.

Now, involve all three senses in your *Ananda Gandha* experience. Let your *Ananda Gandha* see, let your *Ananda gandha* hear, let your *Ananda Gandha* taste.

Next involve your touch sense. Involve the whole skin in the *Ananda Gandha* experience – where your skin is touching your clothes, where your hair is playing with your face, where your body is touching the chair, where your crossed legs are touching each other. Just involve the whole touch sense into your *Ananda Gandha* experience. If you feel like touching your body, you can touch it, and involve yourself deeply in this experience. But feel the experience from *Ananda Gandha* as the *Ananda Gandha* experience.

Now involve all four of the senses. Let the experience of all of your four senses become the *Ananda Gandha* experience. Let your *Ananda Gandha* experience all four senses: seeing, hearing, tasting and touching. Let *Ananda Gandha* experience all four sensual experiences simultaneously. Involving the senses in *Ananda Gandha* is what actual sense (intelligence) is. It is *sense*.

Involve your smelling sense next. So many kinds of smells exist around us. We are not even aware of them. We never stay in *Ananda Gandha*.

If you stay in *Ananda Gandha*, without your involvement, you will sense the scent of things in the same way that you see a hundred objects when you open your eyes. You will sense, you will smell so many things around you. Now fold your smelling sense into the *Ananda Gandha* experience. You will smell so many divine fragrances that exist around you.

Actually this very area where you are sitting is heaven. If you are in *Ananda Gandha*, wherever you are sitting will become heaven. If you are not in *Ananda Gandha*, even if you are sitting in a palace, you will experience it as just an ordinary place. Be in *Ananda Gandha* and allow the experience to travel through all the senses. Let all five sense experiences become the one *Ananda Gandha* experience. Involve all your five senses inside *Ananda Gandha*. Let *Ananda Gandha* experience all five senses simultaneously.

With all the five sense experiences, allow the awareness to penetrate your bones, hair, nerves, blood vessels, tissue and internal organs. Move your body with this expanded *Ananda Gandha* awareness, with this expanded bliss experience. Walk slowly with the *Ananda Gandha* awareness. Go and eat with the *Ananda Gandha* awareness. Whatever you eat, whatever you take inside, let everything go to *Ananda Gandha*.

Even the very eating – let *Ananda Gandha* eat it. As of now, your mind is eating. Now walk from *Ananda Gandha*, eat from *Ananda Gandha*, drink from *Ananda Gandha*. If you do all your activities from *Ananda Gandha*, you will see that *Ananda Gandha* will do all the activities. You will sense a new intelligence, a new sensitivity, a new discovery, a new bliss experience continuously.

PRANAMAYA KOSHA MEDITATION

THE PRANIC SYSTEM

We have a clearly defined *prana* (life force energy) flow in our bodies. Just as the nervous system exists, a clear *pranic* system exists. In the *vedic* (Vedas – ancient Hindu scriptures) system they classify it as 72,000 *nadis* (energy pathways).

The main energy pathways are what the Chinese acupuncture system defines as meridians. They are like the energy highways in the body, where the *pranic* flow is high.

The 700 main energy pathways form the main acupuncture points in the acupuncture healing system. These 700 points are the major junctions of the 72,000 *nadis*.

We are not able to feel these energy pathways because we are not aware of our *pranic* flow. We have become so insensitive that we cannot sense the oxygen coming in and going out.

As of now you are conscious. You are able to see this physical body. If you sleep, you go to the unconscious state and you are not able to see this body. From the unconscious state, when your frequency increases and when it touches the conscious, that is when you are able to sense this body itself. That is when you become aware of it. Otherwise, you can't even sense this physical body. In the same way, when you increase your awareness to the super-conscious level, then you will see that the *pranic* body exists around and inside you.

Pranamaya Kosha Meditation technique

This meditation is to live in *Ananda Gandha* at the *pranic* or breath level.

Start living in *Ananda Gandha*. Expand your awareness to the nostrils. Along with the inhaled air, the very life force, the *prana* also comes in. Don't put too much effort into experiencing it. Just be aware. Allow the inhalation to happen. Don't try to alter it. Just witness. Whatever happens, let it happen.

Just as how you inhale through the nostrils, with the same feeling, start inhaling from your toes. Forget about everything else. Let *Ananda Gandha* be the end of the nostrils. Let the toes become the opening of the nostrils. Just inhale and exhale. If you feel the cross-legged pose is not working, you can relax your legs. Start inhaling from the toes. Let the toes inhale. Let the toes exhale. Visualize this. You will feel and see that the toes are inhaling *prana* and exhaling *prana*.

Let *Ananda Gandha* be the end of the nostrils. Let both the left and right legs inhale and exhale. Visualize that both the legs are inhaling *prana* and exhaling *prana*. Let the *prana* touch *Ananda Gandha* and then let it go.

Now include the *muladhara* area. Inhale *prana* and exhale *prana*. Let the blissful *pranic* energy come inside your body and spread all over the body.

Now allow the whole spinal cord to inhale and exhale. Let the whole abdomen and chest along with the spinal cord inhale *prana* and exhale *prana*.

See the multiple openings of the body. See *prana* entering into the numerous openings existing in the abdomen and chest and spinal cord. Let the whole *prana* come to *Ananda Gandha* and then spread to the whole body and then let it go out.

Now inhale through both the hands. Let the hands inhale *prana* through the tips of the ten fingers. Let *Ananda Gandha* inhale the *prana* through the hands.

Now, inhale through all the openings existing in your head. Next, let the whole face inhale *prana* and exhale *prana*; through the ears, through the eyelids, through the forehead, through the tongue, through the lips, through the skin on the face. Let *Ananda Gandha* inhale *prana* and exhale *prana* through the face.

Now combine all five steps and allow the whole body to inhale and exhale. Let the center of your body, *Ananda Gandha,* inhale *prana* through the whole body and let your body be rejuvenated. Let *prana* go out through the whole body. Feel the blissful vibrations. Feel the enormous energy that is coming in and going out with each inhalation and exhalation.

EFFECT OF EMOTIONS ON THE STRUCTURE OF DNA

At the Institute of HeartMath, some experiments have been conducted on the effect of emotions on various biological parameters ranging from Heart Rate Variability (HRV) to DNA structure.

In one experiment, some human placenta (the most pristine form of DNA) was placed in a container from which they could measure changes in the DNA. Twenty-eight researchers were each given a vial of DNA. Each researcher had been trained in generating and experiencing feelings. The researchers introduced various emotions into the DNA and found that the DNA changed its shape according to the emotions expressed. When love, gratitude and appreciation were expressed, the DNA responded by relaxing and the strands unwound. The DNA became longer.

When the researchers felt anger, fear, frustration or stress, the DNA responded by tightening up. It became shorter, and many of the DNA codes switched off!

The shut-down of the DNA codes was reversed, and the codes were switched back on again when feelings of love, joy, gratitude and appreciation were introduced. This experiment was later followed up with HIV positive patients. Feelings of love, gratitude and appreciation increased the resistance in these patients by 300,000 times.

> Living in *Ananda Gandha* will work beyond the emotions. It will not only relax the DNA, but will rejuvenate, reshape and rebuild the DNA towards divinity. That means it will change your whole physiology and psychology towards the permanent state of bliss. It will not only take you to a different timeline, it will take you beyond time itself.

Collective Consciousness

Chapter 30
Collective Consciousness

To really understand the significance of the service you healers have been initiated into, you have to know some fundamental, deep Truths about life itself.

First thing, all our minds are not individual separate pieces of the universe. They are all one and the same. All our minds are interlinked. Not only interlinked, they directly affect each other. This is what I call 'Collective Consciousness'.

If you catch a cold from someone, you might suffer physically for a few days and then finally get over it. But when you catch thoughts from people, not only do you suffer mentally but the suffering is forever. Similarly, anything you think affects the people staying around you. It not only affects those who are staying around you but everyone living on planet earth is touched by your thoughts.

Any of my thoughts can transform you. Any of your thoughts can touch me. We are not separate individuals. There is only one thing called collective consciousness.

You are connected not only at the mental level, but even at the deeper conscious levels. The deeper you go, the deeper you experience that you are connected.

We don't have just this physical body. We have seven energy bodies. We are all connected in the levels of all the seven energy bodies (Figure 6).

Collective Consciousness

Now, in the physical layer, you, God and I can be represented as three different points in the concentric circle, quite far from each other. In the physical layer, the distance is too much.

If you come down to the *pranic* or breath body, the distance is reduced. If you come down deeper to the mental level, the distance between you and I is further reduced and so is the distance between you and God. When you travel deeper and deeper and finally reach the *nirvanic* or bliss body, these three entities finally merge into one. At the deep end of all these layers, God, you, and I are One. There is no distance.

All of us think that we own our intellectual identity. However the simple truth is that, in actual existence, no such thing as a separate individual identity exists. Once we know this truth, we go beyond pain, suffering, depression and disease. Understand clearly, that as long as we have this concept of individual identity, physically or mentally or at the being level, we will be continuously suffering.

If you fall in tune with the Whole, the Whole behaves as your friend. The moment you start thinking or behaving in opposition with the Whole, it starts acting like an enemy. The Whole, the universe, is a hologram of which we are a part. Just as in a hologram, every single part of the hologram, even if split, reflects the totality of that hologram, we reflect the totality of the Whole that is the universe.

Wherever we want to achieve success, whether in the social or economic world, when we tune in with the whole group and fall in tune with the collective consciousness, we will achieve whatever it is that we want to achieve.

If we disappear into the collective consciousness, we will be protected and taken care of again and again. We will attain complete success, not only socially and economically, but we will also experience a feeling of fulfillment which is inexplicable.

As long as we resist the current, whether it is in our workplace, our house, our company or any other place for that matter, as long as we do not disappear into the collective consciousness, we will be continuously creating hell for ourselves and for others.

Seeds of violence are created whenever we feel we are an individual, unconnected or unrelated to others. We become selfish, dogmatic and violent. With individual consciousness, we dissect, we cut things into pieces and such logic always breaks. However, with collective consciousness, we unify.

First of all, remember that at the physical level, we are not independent individuals. Our body and the body of the sun and the moon are connected. Any small change in the body of the sun can make changes in our body. Any small change in our body can change the body of the moon and vice versa. Some of us may have noticed that the phases of the moon affect the state of our mind.

In the mental layer also we are not alone. At any given point of time, any thought rising from anyone else's head, comes and touches us and any thought created in our mind goes and touches someone else. This is going on continuously.

Thoughts are like ripples created on the surface of a lake. If we create a strong wave, we will be creating an impression with our thoughts. We will be leading and inspiring others with our thoughts. However, if our thoughts are not solid enough, other waves will impress us.

Either we live as leaders or as followers. There is no in-between. Either you lead or you follow!

Finally, at the spiritual level, the moment we understand that we are deeply, totally and intensely connected to the whole group, to the whole universe, not only do we start experiencing bliss, but we also really start living. This opening up leads to the opening up of many different amazing dimensions of our being.

Our Thoughts Affect the Very Structure of Water

Our thoughts and energy flow have the capacity to create and attract incidents and people who are of a similar nature. There is a beautiful research that demonstrates this:

A Japanese doctor, Masaru Emoto, has done beautiful research on water and published the results of his findings in a book called, 'Hidden Messages from Water.' As a scientist, he works on different possibilities, exploring the power of mind over matter or mind's influence on matter and how the energetic vibration of one thing, whether subtle or gross, affects the energy expression of water.

He took ten cups of water from the same source and kept them in ten different rooms under the same conditions such as temperature, etc.

Each day, he spent time in each room. In one room, he would create some positive thoughts like peace, bliss or joy for five minutes and then leave the room. He would then go to the next room and create some violent thoughts like war, terrorism, violence and anger. He would then go to the third room, and chant some words from the Dhammapada, Buddha's teachings. Next, he froze the water from each of the rooms and took pictures of the water crystals through a microscope.

The images of the water crystals were dramatic and simply shocking. The water crystals from the water near which he used positive words shone beautifully and clearly like a diamond. The water near which he used negative words looked ghostly, dark, dense and disorganized. The water near which he chanted Buddha's teachings formed into a crystal that looked divine. This was not a random result. With over 300 attempts, the same results were replicated. He went on to conduct this experiment using various types of music. The water responded in an integrated or disintegrated way depending upon the type of music played.

This startling research supports Einstein's Theory of Relativity. We are not isolated structures traveling through empty space! We are vibrating energy, constantly changing, interacting and influencing everything, including ourselves! Since our thoughts do affect water in the outer environment, they can and do affect the water and blood that flows in every cell of our bodies, 80% of which is composed of water.

We are the world. We can change and improve the world. We can do it by changing ourselves through the choices we make, the thoughts we entertain and through the decision to make the quantum leap to live continuously in bliss!

Natural Calamities and Collective Negativity

If five minutes of one person's negative thoughts can affect one glass of water, what will happen when so many of us are experiencing so much irritation and negativity? Of course nature will be disturbed! Natural calamities occur because of our collective negativity. When we express so much fear and negativity, where do you think all the energy is deposited? How will it be expressed and dissipated?

One glass of water can become negative energy just by one man's five minutes of negative thoughts over a short period of time. Imagine then, billions of people constantly radiating negativity, negative thoughts, negative words, negative energy. Of course the ocean will be affected. We are abusing nature and ourselves with our negativity. We are creating energy imbalances in nature with our negativity.

Now, as Nithya Spiritual Healers, you can do something constructive to reduce the collective negativity and raise the collective consciousness. By doing *Ananda Gandha* meditation and being in tune with cosmic energy, you are lowering the negative consciousness and raising the level of collective positive energy.

With every breath that you take in, be in *Ananda Gandha*. Inhale the negativity; it will simply disappear as it touches the ultimate source of energy in *Ananda Gandha*. Exhale the bliss that is bubbling every moment inside you in *Ananda Gandha*.

DECIDE YOUR DESTINY!

To conclude, a small story:

One day all the employees of a company reached the office and they saw a big notice on the door saying, 'Yesterday the person who has been hindering your growth in this company passed away. Please join us for the funeral service in the conference room.'

Initially all were shocked and saddened at the death of one of their colleagues. Ideas of who it could be crossed everyone's mind. Each employee was curious to see if it was indeed the person that they assumed it to be. The excitement grew in the conference room as everyone filed in and saw an open coffin surrounded by beautiful flowers.

The employees quietly formed a line to pay their respects to their dead colleague. Everyone wondered, 'Who was it who hindered my progress? Who was it that held our company back? Maybe it is good that he died!' The thought of being able to work without unwanted restrictions excited them all.

One by one the thrilled employees got closer to the coffin. When each of them looked inside they were stunned and speechless. They stood nearby, shocked and in silence, as if someone had touched the deepest part of their soul.

Inside the coffin there was no co-worker. There was a mirror. Everyone who looked inside saw only himself!

A small sign next to the mirror read: 'There is only one person who is capable of limiting your growth: YOU!'

You are the only person who can revolutionize your life. You are the only person who can influence your happiness, realize your dreams and your success. You are the only person who can help yourself. Your life does not change when your boss changes, when your friends change, when your parents change, when your partner changes, when your company changes. Your life changes when YOU change. When you choose to go beyond your limiting beliefs, embracing the truth that only you are responsible for your life, a quantum transformation is possible.

The most important relationship you can have is the one you have with yourself. Examine yourself, watch yourself. Become aware of what you are experiencing in the outer and the inner worlds. Don't be afraid of difficulties, seeming impossibilities and losses. Connect with yourself at your core, over and over again until it becomes your way of life. Then you will simply radiate the enlightened qualities of bliss, confidence, compassion and intelligence. You will create a heaven on earth – for yourself and for everyone that you encounter.

May you experience, be one with, and radiate eternal bliss – *Nithyananda*!

Thank you.